Not Angels but Agencies

D0920117

To
members of SMT
1986-95
with gratitude and affection

Michael Taylor

Not Angels but Agencies

The Ecumenical Response to Poverty – A Primer

WAGGONER LIBRARY
DISCARD

WAGGONER LIBRARY
TREVECCA NAZARENE UNIVERSITY

SCM PRESS LTD
WCC Publications, Geneva

Published jointly by SCM Press Ltd., 9-17 St Albans Place, London N1 0NX, England, and WCC Publications, World Council of Churches, 150 route de Ferney, 1211 Geneva 2, Switzerland.

All rights reserved. No part of this publication may be reproduced, stored in a retrieval system or transmitted, in any form or by any means, electronic, mechanical, photocopying, recording or otherwise, without the prior permission of the publishers.

Cover design: Edwin Hassink/WCC

Cover photo: Peter Williams/WCC
Back cover photo: Christian Aid/D.K. Crevance

ISBN WCC 2-8254-1168-X
ISBN SCM 0-334-02624-5

© 1995 WCC Publications

First printing December 1995

Printed and bound in Finland by WSOY

Contents

Preface

Ever since student days I have felt at home in the ecumenical movement. I owe it an enormous debt of gratitude. A book like this cannot even begin to repay it, but it does give me an opportunity to acknowledge it. Like many others, I am not so sure as I once was about where I want the ecumenical movement to go; but I am as sure as ever that I want to be part of it. If we now look further than the unity of the churches to the unity of faiths and of all humankind, we cannot neglect the part, namely the unity of Christians, in our quest for the whole. If we now accept as inevitable and even welcome diversity and disagreement, they have to be characteristics of our unity, not reasons to despair over it. If we are to seek unity for the sake of the poor, we shall hardly be good news to them unless we free each other from the blindness and captivities of our separate churches. And if we are looking for God's truth, we have little hope of finding it except in the company of all God's people.

One of the many lessons the ecumenical movement has tried to teach me is to have wide horizons while keeping my feet on the ground in one particular place or, to put it in its own inimitable language, "think globally, act locally". Over the years, that particular place for me has been a local council of churches, then an ecumenical federation for training in ministry, and, most recently, Christian Aid, the aid and development agency of forty churches in the United Kingdom and Ireland. If in what follows I refer to it more often than to the many other agencies that have contributed to the ecumenical response to poverty, that is not because it is superior to the rest (even if it is superior in my affections) but because I know it well and it seemed wise to anchor what are wide-ranging debates to a place which I know and for which I must take some responsibility.

The usual apologies for "bad language" are in order. The howlers in relation to gender can I hope be excused on historical grounds: that is how we used to talk all the time! "North" and "South", "First World" and "Third World", "developed" and "developing" persist as inaccurate ways of describing the great divide between rich and poor countries. They may soon become out of date as well as misleading, as poverty becomes a global issue and no respecter of geographical boundaries. "Agencies" as used in the title of the book includes not only the so-called donor agencies of the "North", but councils of churches, churches and voluntary organizations worldwide which have been agents of the ecumenical response to poverty, human and flawed, but aspiring to be "angels" or messengers of a Christlike God.

My special personal thanks go to Myra Blyth for her real encouragement; to a number of friends and colleagues, including Jenny Borden, Pamela Gruber, Cees Oskam, Park Kyung-Seo, Ronald Preston, Paul Spray and Wendy Tyndale, who read what I had written and suggested how it could be improved, but who are not of course to be held responsible for the outcome; to Sue Matthews and Judith Knight for word-processing with skill and without complaint; and to Isabel Csupor and Emilia Reichmuth for a great deal of practical help.

Christa Hunzinger made a huge contribution to the enterprise, understanding perfectly the kind of research assistance that I needed and checking seemingly endless documents and references with speed and accuracy to make sure that I got it right.

Michael H. Taylor

1. The Year of the Lord's Favour

The immediate occasion of writing this book is the jubilee year
that almost never was.

The mid-1990s have brought a spate of 50th anniversaries or
jubilees. They have included the 50th birthday of the United Nations,
of international financial institutions like the World Bank and the
International Monetary Fund (IMF), of the principal service arm of the
World Council of Churches, known for many years as CICARWS
(Commission on Inter-Church Aid, Refugee and World Service), and
of organizations like Christian Aid, the ecumenical aid and development agency of forty churches in the United Kingdom and Ireland.

All these organizations have from day one been shot through with
idealism. After the horrors of a world war (1939-45) which killed,
maimed, destroyed, uprooted, bereaved and impoverished, they were
inspired by a vision of a world where such things would not be
repeated, and they were all committed in their various ways to
achieving it.

A world without poverty was one aspect of this vision. Poverty
was much older than the war, of course, but there was a fresh
determination to deal with it, and like the more immediate problem of
refugees in Europe, there were high hopes that it could be overcome.
The movement for world development which sprang up after the war
had in its sights a jubilee which by the 1990s would amount to a great
deal more than being 50 years old or feeling entitled just for once to
blow your own trumpet.

Jubilee is a biblical idea, though the word itself is not mentioned in
the Bible all that often. It was the 50th year after seven "weeks" of
years: seven times seven plus one. The rules for its observance are in
Leviticus 25. As far as we know, it was never put into practice. Even

in the Bible it was "the jubilee year that never was". There are allusions to it in Isaiah; and when Jesus referred in his inaugural sermon in the synagogue in Nazareth (Luke 4) to "the year of the Lord's favour", it is generally assumed he had Isaiah (from whom he lifts a direct quotation) and the jubilee in mind.

Jubilee required the Israelites to take very practical steps indeed to see that once in a while — even if it was a long while — nature got a rest and the poorest got a chance to be free of their debts and free of employers who made them work extraordinarily hard for next to nothing, and to start afresh with something to eat (unharvested crops, for example) and the wherewithal to make a living. Jubilee was all about social justice, redressing the balance between rich and poor, and redistribution, reversing the inevitable drift whereby those who have receive even more, while from those who have not, even the little they have is taken away.

Something of that jubilee vision of a fairer world, where past injustice is put right and desperate poverty is no more and everyone has a reasonable opportunity to earn a living and have a say in what happens to them, inspired the pioneers of 50 years ago. Among them were the ecumenical pioneers involved in what I have called "the ecumenical response to poverty". Who were they, and who are they now?

The ecumenical family

For the purposes of this book the members of the "ecumenical family" most closely involved can be divided into three main groups. In the first are the so-called agencies, of which Christian Aid is one. As we have said, they began to appear in the 1940s in the aftermath of the second world war. They are the agencies of churches in Europe, North America, Australia and New Zealand. They are usually ecumenical in character; in other words, they act for more than one church or as a department or offshoot of a council of churches, and in close cooperation with the World Council of Churches (WCC). They now raise money from their churches, from the public and from governments. They spend it in several ways. They help struggling churches to rebuild or survive. They bring relief to the victims of droughts or floods or earthquakes or wars, including refugees. They support longer-term development programmes which help people to improve their security and the quality of their lives. And they support development education and campaigns in their own countries to inform people about the causes of poverty and how they can help to remove them. Some of the agencies do some of these things; some, including Christian Aid, do almost all of them.

As the main source of funds for the ecumenical response to poverty, these agencies have often been referred to as "donor agencies". There were over 20 of them in 1995.

In 1990 the European agencies formed themselves into an association called APRODEV (association of WCC-related development agencies in Europe). It has an office in Brussels and pays particular attention to the policies and practices of the European Union with regard to relief aid and development.

The second group of family members is made up of councils of churches or Christian councils in Africa, Asia, Latin America, the Caribbean, the Pacific and the Middle East. They number well over 70. Most are national councils. Six are regional councils: the All Africa Conference of Churches (AACC), the Christian Conference of Asia (CCA), the Latin American Council of Churches (CLAI), the Caribbean Conference of Churches (CCC), the Pacific Conference of Churches (PCC) and the Middle East Council of Churches (MECC). Several of them bring churches and councils together over a whole continent. The Conference of European Churches (CEC) spans both East and West.

National councils of churches go back well before the 1940s. One of the oldest, in India, was founded in 1912. If we were to tell their stories here they would be very diverse but with a number of common themes. Their forerunners are the overseas missions of the European and North American churches which made increasing efforts to take counsel with each other and to work together in the field — or at least to avoid treading on one another's toes. The struggles of national councils of churches often reflect the emergence of independent nations from the shadows of colonial rule, and of the "younger churches" into a life of their own. The majority of their members are Protestant and Anglican churches with some Orthodox. There is a growing involvement of Roman Catholics, especially in recent years. Their agendas have covered the whole range of Christian work and witness. They have striven to be "holistic" or rounded in their approach. Councils in Asia have shown a particular concern to combine service and mission.

Aid and development have nevertheless featured prominently in all their programmes, and many councils have created special departments for this purpose. In some cases, such as Christian Care in Zimbabwe and the Church's Auxiliary for Social Action (CASA) in India, these departments became separate ecumenical organizations. The emphasis on aid was due largely to the obvious fact that the councils needed help from outside if they and their member churches were in turn to help their own desperately poor communities. But it was also due to the needs of the Northern agencies and the WCC for known and trusted counterparts, fellow members of the ecumenical movement, who would screen applications for aid and through whom they could channel their funds.

The resulting partnership between the agencies and the councils has not been without its difficulties. Councils can be left with skewed agendas dictated more by the availability of funds and the interests of funding agencies than their own convictions. The agencies which helped to foster them for their own good reasons can turn to other organizations, including secular ones, when it suits them, insisting that effective development must come before ecumenical relations. For all the talk of self-reliance, councils of churches can remain in a state of dependency, unable or not allowed to support themselves. They can be pushed beyond their resources. They can be criticized for not managing their affairs as others deem they should. Like all ecumenical bodies, including the agencies, they can cut adrift from their members and act instead of their churches rather than enabling their churches to act together.

The third group of family members are to be found within the WCC, especially in CICARWS and what became known in 1992 as Unit IV. The full story of the WCC or even of this part of it cannot be told here,[1] but if the reader is to make sense of what follows and not be confused or simply irritated by a bewildering collection of acronyms, dates and details, then some background information must be given.

From reconstruction to sharing and service

The founding of the WCC in 1948 was not the beginning of the ecumenical movement or of efforts to draw divided Christians and divided churches together. They had already come together to talk about "faith and order" (their different teachings and attitudes to baptism, the eucharist or holy communion and the ordained ministry) and "life and work" (how they worked out their faith in practice). Their young people were already organized into the YMCA (Young Men's Christian Association) and the YWCA (Young Women's Christian Association) and the SCM (Student Christian Movement). First and foremost, their missionaries and mission societies had already heard the call to unity "that the world might believe" and, following a global conference in Edinburgh in 1910, had formed the International Missionary Council (IMC) in 1921. When the WCC was born it was late in time, waiting for ten years after it was conceived, mainly under the shadow of war.

In 1938, when W.A. Visser 't Hooft was invited to become the WCC's first general secretary, he accepted on condition that the Council would become active in the field of aid, because "there could be no healthy ecumenical fellowship without practical solidarity".[2] A Provisional Committee began meeting in 1942, and the inaugural assembly of the member churches was held in Amsterdam in 1948. The IMC became a full part of the WCC in 1961.

The theme of the first assembly was "Man's Disorder and God's Design". Six more assemblies have followed: in 1954 (Evanston: "Christ — The Hope of the World"), 1961 (New Delhi: "Jesus Christ — The Light of the World"), 1968 (Uppsala: "Behold, I Make All Things New"), 1975 (Nairobi: "Jesus Christ Frees and Unites"), 1983 (Vancouver: "Jesus Christ — The Life of the World") and 1991 (Canberra: "Come, Holy Spirit — Renew the Whole Creation"). In 1998 the assembly is to meet in Harare, under the theme "Turn to God — Rejoice in Hope".

The assembly in Canberra noted that "through the six preceding assemblies the WCC has called the attention of its member churches... to serious contradictions and imbalances prevailing in the world economic system" and that "since the first assembly the WCC has repeatedly emphasized that there is an urgent need to review the existing world economic order".[3] That may well be true, but it was the Uppsala assembly "which took the force of the wave of anti-racist, anti-colonialist feeling"[4] and will be remembered for speaking the loudest. Almost at the outset of its message it acknowledged that "we heard the cry of those who long for peace; of the hungry and exploited who demand bread and justice; of the victims of discrimination who claim human dignity". It went on to say that "the ever-widening gap between the rich and the poor, fostered by armament expenditure, is the crucial point of decision today".[5]

Assemblies receive reports on the work of the Council and its staff and give guidance for the future. Two of the Council's many and varied departments have been especially identified with the ecumenical response to poverty.

The first began life in 1944 as the Department of Reconstruction. Its major task was to help the war-stricken churches of Europe. From the outset it adopted a three-part pattern of working which has remained familiar ever since. It set up or contacted committees and councils of churches and their agencies in countries which could offer help (first in the USA, Britain, Switzerland, Denmark and Sweden; later in Canada, New Zealand and Australia). It asked the non-Catholic churches in war-stricken countries to set up national committees to discuss their common needs (in France, Belgium, the Netherlands, Norway, Germany, Poland, Austria, Czechoslovakia and Hungary). The Department was the link between the other two parties, matching needs with resources and offers of help. It also undertook special pieces of work or "projects" in its own name through funds sent directly to the WCC headquarters in Geneva. Already we see the three groups of members of the ecumenical family at work, even if at this stage they were almost all in the Northern countries.

By 1945 the Department had been united with the older European Central Bureau for Inter-Church Aid (1922) and renamed the Department of Reconstruction and Inter-Church Aid. It was to continue to deal with material aid but concentrate more and more on "inter-church aid", which meant helping churches with "their spiritual tasks".[6] By 1949 it had taken on the work of the Ecumenical Refugee Commission set up in 1946 and was given yet another name: Department of Inter-Church Aid and Service to Refugees (DICASR).

As the immediate post-war problems of Europe receded, DICASR began to look further afield, no doubt stimulated by the first meeting of the WCC central committee outside the Western world, in Lucknow, India, in 1952-53. It received an official mandate from the Evanston assembly to work in Africa, Asia and Latin America. The new mandate raised practical and theological questions about cooperating with the IMC, which had long-established links through the missionary societies with all these parts of the world. The geographical change also brought a change in emphasis from rehabilitating churches in Europe to their former standards of relative prosperity to supporting poor and mostly minority churches in poor countries. The Department's name was changed to "Division".

Projects

In 1956 DICASR published its first "project list": a register of defined pieces of work with budgets or price-tags attached. As time went on these projects covered a whole range of work from emergency relief to development. Intended to encourage self-reliance and good ecumenical relations, they were run by the churches and church-related organizations but for the benefit of the wider community. They were screened and recommended by national councils of churches in the South and approved and listed for funding by the WCC.

"Priority projects" were introduced in 1971 and treated differently. Instead of simply being listed by Geneva as suitable for funding, leaving the agencies to pick and choose among them, priority projects were guaranteed 90 percent of the money required out of central, unearmarked ecumenical funds — which in fact came from much the same sources.

As the project list became a major feature of the life and work of DICASR and its successors, it was inevitably the subject of considerable debate. It took up a great deal of the time of WCC staff, yet it only accounted for less than 10 percent of the funds flowing from North to South. The procedures for listing and deciding were slow, encouraging those who needed money and those who needed to spend it to bypass the WCC in Geneva and deal directly with one another. For many the list embodied all that was wrong with aid in general. It was therefore swept up into the larger ongoing debates about mission and development, politics and power — the subjects of subsequent chapters of this book. The "church of the poor", it was claimed, which serves its equals in humility and with deep love, "is beyond the list of projects of agencies". [7]

As early as 1971 the replacement of the project list by "a deeper and more real partnership in the whole business of sharing resources" was being mooted, and in 1973 the abolition of the list was proposed.

In 1975, however, the Nairobi assembly reaffirmed it "as an essential instrument". After renewed criticism at the WCC world consultation on Inter-Church Aid, Refugee and World Service in Larnaca, Cyprus, in 1986, CICARWS (the successor to DICASR) took steps to end its involvement in listing and screening projects. This still did not spell the end of the project list. Priority projects continued. The rest were not abandoned but handed over to the agencies, now judged best able to deal with them: "CICARWS' strong... involvement with projects may have been justified 20 years ago. Today, the churches of the North operate through specialized agencies which handle a multiple of funds with a multiple of experienced and competent staff compared with CICARWS."[8] Meanwhile CICARWS increasingly turned its attention to what was called the Ecumenical Sharing of Resources and the systems for sharing that went with it.

The 1960s saw two significant shifts in the work of DICASR. The first, authorized by the WCC central committee in New Delhi, widened the project list to include projects which went beyond the immediate relief of need to tackle its causes. This was not patching things up but "development" towards a better state of affairs. The first two projects were in India and Chile. During the first Development Decade proclaimed by the United Nations, the number and range of development projects rapidly expanded into agriculture, medicine, education and social work.

The second shift at New Delhi was from Europe to the Third World, turning outwards from an inter-church enterprise mainly helping churches to one which strengthened the churches for Christian service (*diakonia* in Greek) to the wider world community: "to help meet the needs on behalf of humanity and without distinction of creed, caste, race, nationality or politics". A fourth new name reflected the shift: Division of Inter-Church Aid, Refugee and World Service (DICARWS).

In the 1960s, and especially at a conference in Swanwick, England, in 1966 (in preparation for the WCC's world conference on Church and Society in Geneva later that year), DICARWS began to talk seriously about tackling social and economic injustice. There would be growing confrontation over the years between different concepts of development or, more accurately, ways of overcoming poverty. They surfaced in Geneva in 1966 and again at the Uppsala assembly in 1968. According to one concept, the economic and technical progress of the Western industrialized countries would be shared with the rest of the world and would raise living standards all around. This was "development". According to the other, this kind of "progress" only led to the under-development of poorer countries and their growing dependence on the rich. The poor did not benefit. They were only exploited. The answer lay in gaining their freedom. They must not be dependent. They must take the future into their own hands. This was "liberation" or "revolution".

One result of this confrontation, to a large extent between the First World and the Third, was a fresh look at what the WCC meant by "development". A consultation in Montreux, Switzerland, in 1970 on "Ecumenical Assistance to Development Projects" called on the WCC to set up a special commission on development; and the Commission on the Churches' Participation in Development (CCPD) began life that same year.[9] The two departments of the WCC especially identified with the ecumenical response to poverty, DICARWS and CCPD, were meant to complement and cooperate with each other. CCPD was to coordinate a comprehensive approach to development — an approach which insisted on social justice but initially remained optimistic about technical progress and economic growth — while DICARWS concentrated, though not exclusively, on immediate needs.

In 1971 the WCC central committee decided to simplify the WCC's internal structure. It set up three programme units and DICARWS (now CICARWS) became part of Unit II along with CCPD, the Commission of the Churches on International Affairs (CCIA), the Programme to Combat Racism (PCR) and, after 1977, the Christian Medical Commission (CMC). The unit was given a nicely balanced title: Justice and Service.

Sharing resources

The ecumenical sharing of resources came to dominate the thinking of CICARWS after the Nairobi assembly of 1975. After several consultations on the subject, responsibility for it was transferred in 1983 from CICARWS to a new Office for Resource Sharing, based within the WCC general secretariat, in recognition of its relevance to many other areas of the Council's work. The Vancouver assembly that year made resource sharing a priority, and in 1985 the WCC central committee agreed to a world consultation on it: "Koinonia: Sharing Life in a World Community", held at El Escorial, Spain, in 1987. Responsibility for resource sharing was returned to the programme unit on Sharing and Service (Unit IV), the successor to CICARWS in the WCC's internal reorganization of 1992.

The ecumenical sharing of resources was designed to supersede the more traditional ways of giving and receiving resources typified by the project list. Its essential features are three. First, sharing was to be more equal. All would be givers and all receivers. All would be "haves" and "have nots". The old donor mentality was to go. Second, resources were to be understood not only as material, but were to include spiritual, theological and cultural resources, as well as personnel. This broader understanding is not only right but necessary, since without it there would be little or nothing in most cases to reciprocate. Third, more people were to have a chance to make decisions or at least to have a share in making them. Poor people, women and young people were to be included. Responsibility was to be devolved. Within the ecumenical family that meant chiefly to "regional groups" (a process often referred to as "regionalization"), which CICARWS set up in the early 1970s in Africa, Asia, Latin America and the Caribbean, the Middle East and Europe and later in the Pacific.

Originally these regional groups were designed to help with screening and listing projects. In 1982 the WCC issued its first *Resource Sharing Book* and by 1983 regional resource-sharing groups had been formed. After Larnaca and El Escorial they were redesigned and given a new brief: to analyze the needs of a region and agree on the parameters within which all the sharing of resources, whether through the WCC or not, should then take place. The decisive voice was to be the local voice. Round tables, to which we shall come, were encouraged to take on similar responsibilities at the national level, and the two together — regional groups and round tables — became the mainstays of the resource-sharing system. Faithfulness to the guidelines for sharing drawn up at El Escorial and respect for the guidance given by regional groups and round tables were part of what came to be known as "ecumenical discipline".

As we have seen, CICARWS' own major world consultation was held in 1986, a year before El Escorial. Larnaca had its own agenda. It emphasized the wide-ranging nature of *diakonia* or Christian service, which should include far more than material help; and it stressed the importance of the local church as the main agent of Christian service. But Larnaca also echoed many of the concerns of the ongoing discussion about resource sharing. Looking back, it seems strange that these two major events, Larnaca and El Escorial, came so close together: "it has been difficult from the outset to see any clear distinction between the main thrusts of the two world consultations on interchurch aid and ecumenical sharing." [10]

Marking the 50th anniversary in 1994 of what was now the WCC's Unit IV, Sharing and Service, the WCC central committee saw its future work in terms of ensuring that the many and varied resources of the churches and their agencies "are brought together, not only into a well-coordinated programme of practical church action, but also into a global strategy for change". [11]

Refugees

From the start, refugees have been at the centre of the ecumenical agenda in the field of aid; indeed, as we have seen, they were one of the main reasons for beginning this involvement. Over the years, the number of refugees has grown rather than diminished.

Even before the WCC Refugee Service was founded in 1944, ecumenical help had been given to Christians fleeing from Nazi Germany; and the IMC had insisted that it be given equally to Christians and Jews. Evidently this had not been entirely the case: "endemic anti-Semitism was tacitly recognized in the emphasis placed on the help to non-Aryan Christians in all the ecumenical efforts". [12] In 1946 the Refugee Service became part of the Department for Reconstruction, and by 1949 was completely integrated into the new DICASR, where it has remained ever since.

The WCC was one of the first international organizations to work closely with the United Nations High Commissioner for Refugees (UNHCR) when that office replaced the IRO (International Refugee Organization) in 1951. In 1986 it helped to set up the International Ecumenical Consultative Committee on Refugees (IECCR) to improve cooperation between the WCC and its related agencies and their Roman Catholic counterparts such as Caritas Internationalis and the International Catholic Migration Committee (ICMC). A Global

Ecumenical Network, drawing together the many and varied ministries to refugees of the WCC member churches, was formed in 1992. In 1995 the WCC central committee adopted a major new policy statement entitled "A Moment to Choose: Risking to Be with Uprooted People".

While ecumenical service to refugees has always had a strong life and an extensive agenda of its own, its boundaries have never been easy to define. The difficulty is reflected in the growing list of terms: refugees, migrants, asylum-seekers, internally displaced, economic refugees, uprooted people. According to the working definition produced by a WCC consultation on refugee resettlement in Stony Point, USA, in 1981:

> Refugees are those who are forced to leave their homes and who are unable or unwilling to return because of persecution or well-founded fear of persecution, for reasons of race, religion, ethnicity, nationality, membership in a particular social group, political opinion, systemic economic deprivation, or because of war-related circumstances. [13]

The causes that create refugees and the causes that create poverty are much the same. So are the debates about what adds up to an adequate ecumenical response. For example, the point about meeting immediate needs but also removing underlying causes (see Chapter 3) is repeated here as often as it is elsewhere. And there is the same historical pattern, beginning in Europe but soon broadening out to the Middle East, Africa, Asia and Latin America.

So perhaps we may be allowed to include refugees in a single discussion about the ecumenical response to poverty, remembering that they suffer one of its extreme consequences, forced as they are to leave their homes; and that they remain one of its most extreme cases. In the words of Larnaca, refugees "are like a mirror through whose suffering we can see the injustices, the oppression and maltreatment of the powerless by the powerful". [14]

CCPD

We saw earlier that the WCC set up the Commission on the Churches' Participation in Development in 1970 in response to increasing questions about the notion of development and a desire to deal with it in a more comprehensive way than DICARWS was ever intended to do. CCPD soon repented of its early optimism about what economic development, growth and technology could do for the poor. While devoting considerable resources to development education, it became increasingly sceptical that the rich, however well educated, would ever give up their privileges. By the time of the second consultation between CICARWS and CCPD in Montreux in 1974, it had moved to the settled view that what was required was not aid but structural change towards a more just and participatory society, and that change would come about not by the rich being charitable towards the poor, but by the poor taking matters into their own hands. The action of people themselves or "people's participation" became the hallmark of CCPD's understanding of development, or rather, liberation; and one of its most important activities was to foster networks linking and mobilizing people's movements all over the world.

During the 1970s, CCPD initiated a programme of action and reflection examining the growing estrangement between the church and the poor, going back to the industrial revolution in the North and the colonial period, and challenging the churches to overcome it. Three books were published: *Good News to the Poor* (1977), *Separation without Hope* (1978) and *Towards a Church of the Poor* (1979). A summary document was presented to the WCC central committee in 1980. [15]

In 1978, CCPD brought together economists and ethicists to form an Advisory Group on Economic Matters. Rather than offering technical advice to projects and programmes, it soon began to criticize the existing economic order and develop a principled basis for a new one. In this and other discussions, international financial institutions like the World Bank and transnational corporations — "the dominant institutional form of capitalism today" — came under review and proposals were put forward for their reform. [16] The search for alternative ways of organizing the world led CCPD to give a good deal of its attention to debates about the "New International Economic Order", a "Just, Participatory and Sustainable Society" and, after the Vancouver assembly in 1983, "Justice, Peace and the Integrity of Creation".

CCPD was instrumental in setting up round tables and consortia, later transferred to CICARWS. In 1992, CCPD as such ceased to exist. Its work became part of the remit of the WCC's newly formed Unit III: Justice, Peace and Creation.

Some other members of the family

1. The *Ecumenical Church Loan Fund* (ECLOF), founded in 1946, became part of the Department of Reconstruction and Inter-Church Aid in 1948. Originally it made low-interest loans to needy churches in Europe. By the late 1950s it had broadened its horizons to include Asia, Africa and Latin America, and in 1970 it began supporting grassroots development work as well as church-related programmes.

2. The *Commission of the Churches on International Affairs* (CCIA) was set up in 1946 as a joint commission of the WCC and the IMC. It had a wide-ranging agenda including peace, disarmament, international law and human rights. After the Geneva conference on Church and Society in 1966 it paid a good deal of attention to the problems of the Third World and the international economic order, insisting that existing international economic structures had to be transformed into a "new, just, alternative system".[17]

3. The *Department on Church and Society* was founded immediately after the 1954 Evanston assembly to encourage Christians and churches in Africa, Asia, Latin America and the West to clarify their responsibilities "towards areas of rapid social change", especially in the non-Western world. In 1962 the department began a three-year study programme in preparation for the 1966 Geneva conference. Two years later, the Uppsala assembly adopted most of the conclusions of the Geneva conference. Over 40 percent of those present at Geneva — unusual in those days — were from Africa, Asia and Latin America. The deliberate decision was taken not to ask for delegates. The conference was to speak *to* the churches, not on their behalf. The result was a sharp confrontation, continued at Uppsala, between those who put their faith in the spread of Western technology and indus-trialization to raise living standards all round, and those who believed that nothing short of revolutionary change would do if justice were ever to come about. For the latter the discussion at Geneva about a "responsible society" sounded too much like a defence of Western society and the status quo.

4. The *Division on World Mission and Evangelism* was formed in 1961 after the New Delhi assembly when the International Missionary Council (IMC), itself a parent body of the ecumenical movement, joined the WCC. It became the Commission on World Mission and

Evangelism (CWME) in 1971. It organized several world conferences, among which the one in Melbourne in 1980, on the theme "Your Kingdom Come", understood mission very clearly in terms of solidarity with the poor and the oppressed.

5. *Urban Industrial Mission*, which began life in 1964 as part of DWME, encouraged ministry and mission in urban and industrial areas by supporting local action groups and putting them in contact with each other. In 1978 urban and rural mission joined forces in *Urban Rural Mission* (URM), which insisted that any such mission and evangelism must include the struggle of poor people to change unjust structures of whatever sort: political, economic, social, cultural and religious.

6. *SODEPAX*, the Joint Committee on Society, Development and Peace, was an instrument of collaboration between the WCC and the Roman Catholic Church. Formed in 1968, it set up a number of programmes and organized international conferences in Europe, Africa and Asia. At one of these, in Cartigny, Switzerland, in 1969, Gustavo Gutiérrez read a paper on the meaning of development, which he later reworked into his influential book *Theology of Liberation*. Since underdevelopment was the by-product of the development of other countries, the aim of the poor and the rich was not to be part of the development movement but to be free from it. In 1972 SODEPAX began to study the probable scale and nature of poverty in the year 2000. The results were published in 1975 in Charles Elliott's book *Patterns of Poverty in the Third World*. The collaboration between the WCC and the Roman Catholic Church proved quite difficult, and the staff, budget and programmes of SODEPAX were much reduced in 1972. Nevertheless it ventured on, "in search of a new society" (a programme launched in 1976) and into inter-religious dialogue on hunger and development. SODEPAX was dissolved in 1980.

Ecumenical formation

Here then is the ecumenical family inspired by the jubilee vision of a world which fulfils the biblical injunction and "provides for the poor" (Leviticus 25). One good reason for telling its story is to contribute to what has been called ecumenical formation. As time passes, there is an inevitable loss of ecumenical experience and memory. The family continually welcomes new members, among them new members of staff in the agencies, who have little experience of ecumenical affairs. They have no first-hand experience of those heady days when the ecumenical movement seemed to be "the great new fact of our time". They share its Christian idealism even though many find the church as an institution quite difficult to live with. They bring fresh vigour, not least because they ask awkward questions. They want to do their best for the poorest. They wonder whether it is always achieved through what has been called the "special relation-ship" between agencies and councils of churches. To their minds that relationship often hinders rather than helps. It takes priority over efficient and effective development work. To them it seems sensible to cut free from the cumbersome procedures and mixed agendas of the churches and work with people not primarily because they belong to ecumenical circles but because, regardless of what circles they belong to, they are best qualified to get on with the job. This urge to put efficiency before ecumenism can colour and sour relationships. Coun-cils of churches, their members and representatives, can be treated with lofty impatience and, as they often feel, with disrespect.

It is easy to mount a counter-attack against such attitudes, but that is not at present the point. Nor is the point that if only the newcomers knew a little more ecumenical history they would never adopt these attitudes and arguments in the first place. Some of what they say — history or no history — may well be valid. The point is that they need to get to know the family they are dealing with; otherwise, their attitudes and arguments will not be so much right or wrong as ill-informed, inappropriate and, worst of all, insensitive. They will simply trample unhelpfully where angels fear to tread.

The best way to get to know the family is of course to meet and talk and do things together. Formation takes time and experience, and that is not always feasible. So I have thought of this book as a "primer" or "textbook". It is not a substitute for meeting or for experience, but for many of its pages it offers straightforward, basic information in the hope that the less-experienced who read and assimilate it will not feel domesticated into agreement but will at least know what they are dealing with and avoid the crudest mistakes. They will find here no confident prescriptions for the future, but having read it they may feel more ready to start taking responsibility for it.

But assimilating 50 years of family history is not an easy matter. Dozens of Christian traditions are involved, countless family get-togethers in meetings and consultations, over 70 countries with their own stories to tell and churches to tell them, thousands of parishes and congregations and local communities, and countless interesting individuals. No one can make much use of all that — much less do justice to it.

One good way to get to know a family is by listening to its conversations or, better still, its arguments. Having listened you may not know all that has happened or remember everything that was said, but you will know what matters to it and makes it tick, and that will probably stay in your mind and affect the way you relate to it in the future.

So what follows is in no sense a blow-by-blow account of what happened to the ecumenical family: first and second and third, with dates and places and names. It does not even mention most of the great and colourful characters who have had such an enormous influence on the ecumenical response to poverty — Robert Mackie, the "father" of CICARWS, C.I. Itty of CCPD, Janet Lacey, the first director of Christian Aid, to name but three. What follows is an attempt to go back over the ground and listen to the arguments and rehearse the big thematic debates. To the family's credit they are mostly about religion and politics, the two great subjects the English are warned not to talk about if they want unruffled social relationships — they are too important to maintain an easy peace.

Once again, however, listening to arguments, like assimilating 50 years of history, is easier said than done. If myriads of people are involved in the story, it sometimes seems as though there are almost as many documents. They are not easy to read. Their language, born of brave attempts to communicate above a babel of tongues, does not help. They are not all terribly interesting or inspiring. It is hard to see the wood for the trees. It is easy to get lost in the detail and lose the thread. The decision to listen to the arguments does, however, offer us a principle of selection. The obvious place to listen is where the argumentative actually meet and talk. That suggests leaving to one side most of the separate documents produced by the different groups of family members — the councils of churches and the agencies — and concentrating attention on the "ecumenical documents" as I have called them. These are mainly produced by all three groups when meeting together, often under the auspices of the WCC, in joint commissions, conferences and consultations.

Are the churches working well together?

There is a second reason for telling the story of the ecumenical response to poverty. If there is wisdom to be gained from the past, we need to gather it up as best we can with an eye to the future.

Here we can learn from the negative as well as the positive. As I have read the documents, I have learned a good deal. My own prejudices have been given a few healthy jolts. To take one example, missionary movements these days are easily regarded as behind the times. But the ecumenical documents remind us over and over again of just how far ahead of the times these movements have been, not only as vanguards of the overall ecumenical movement but also in their contributions to the arguments that have surrounded the ecumenical response to poverty. Their views on partnership, sharing, mission, an end to dependency and solidarity with the poor have often in fact been well ahead of the rest.

On the other hand, it is sometimes tempting to reply to the question "What have we learned?" with the answer "Not very much". I have deliberately quoted the documents at considerable length, making some parts of this book as much a reader or anthology as a primer or textbook. If the result is a certain weariness, that may be an experience worth registering. One of the reasons for it could be that documents like these, written by committees, find it difficult by their very nature to inspire. But we can also grow weary because they cease to be interesting. They no longer advance the arguments very much. There are notable shifts of emphasis as the debate goes on. Immediate relief must be accompanied by structural change. The funding of projects gives ground to resource-sharing; modernization to participation. Talk of liberation becomes more acceptable than talk of economic development as the Third World raises its voice — a shift that may now be in reverse. Again there is increasing concern for the environment or the "integrity of creation". But it is all too easy to come away with the impression that the family has failed to make much progress in its thinking, and that what was said at a very early date continues to be said over the years and is still being said now.

In so far as that is true, it carries lessons for the future. If the wisdom we can gather up from the past is more limited than we might have hoped for, it will be just as important to ask "How can we learn more?" as to ask "What should we do next?"

Like any book, this one is written from a limited perspective: within the WCC, from the perspective of Unit IV; within the First World-Third World scenario, from the perspective of the North relating to the South rather than the East; within a divided world, from the perspective of the rich rather than the poor; within the wider ecumenical family from the perspective of a Protestant; within the narrower ecumenical family as I have defined it, from the perspective of the agencies and one agency (Christian Aid) in particular; within the multitude of disciplines we need to bring to bear on our calling, from the perspective of a theological educator rather than an expert in development.

One thing we know before we even begin. The ecumenical response to poverty is 50 and more years old but the jubilee has not yet come about. If it was meant to reverse the relentless flow of resources from the have-nots to the haves, it has largely failed. The gap between rich and poor still grows. According to the United Nations' *Human Development Report* for 1992, in 1960 the 20 percent of the world's population living in the richest countries were 30 times better off than the bottom 20 percent. By 1989 the ratio was 60 to 1; and the corresponding ratio for the world's richest billion people and poorest billion people is 150 to 1. The numbers of the poor increase. Millions of them do not hear much good news. Prisoners are still in captivity. The acceptable year of the Lord remains a dream. It is difficult to know what to celebrate or whether to celebrate at all.

Christian Aid in 1995 chose to strike three notes in its own jubilee year. One was a note of celebration of the achievements not of the rich but of the poor. In countless ways and countless places, against count-less odds, with courage, skill and determination, in faith and hope they have struggled for life. The second was a note of sorrow: a vigil and silent watching over a world where poverty and injustice are still very much at home. The third was a note of recommitment to walk and work with God towards a world where, as Christian Aid chose to put it, "all shall be included in the feast of life". Any book like this is of little use unless it contributes, however modestly, to that end.

Some of what follows was written in Crêt-Bérard, a friendly and hospitable retreat centre in Switzerland which features more than once in the story of the ecumenical response to poverty. One day a woman on retreat asked what I was reading and writing about. Having heard my reply, she put the disarming question: "And are the churches working together well?" I hardly knew where to begin. As long as the jubilee or "the year of the Lord's favour" seems just as far off, the answer is probably No. But I recognized in her straightforward enquiry the question that I in this book and the ecumenical family in its response to poverty should be asking all the time.

NOTES

[1] The standard two-volume *History of the Ecumenical Movement* (vol. 1, 1517-1948, eds R. Rouse and S.C. Neill, 1954; and vol. 2, 1948-1968, ed. H.E. Fey, 1970) was reprinted, Geneva, WCC, 1993, in a one-volume edition. A wide range of useful information covering later years is found in the *Dictionary of the Ecumenical Movement*, Geneva, WCC, 1991.

[2] In K. Slack, ed., *Hope in the Desert*, Geneva, WCC, 1986, p.9.

[3] M. Kinnamon, ed., *Signs of the Spirit*, Geneva, WCC, 1991, p.76.

[4] D.M. Paton, ed., *Breaking Barriers*, Geneva, WCC, 1976, p.4.

[5] N. Goodall, ed., *Uppsala 68 Speaks*, Geneva, WCC, 1968, p.5.

[6] Minutes of the WCC Central Committee meeting, 1949, p.119.

[7] Julio de Santa Ana, ed., *Towards a Church of the Poor*, Geneva, WCC, 1979, p.209.

[8] Minutes of the CICARWS commission meeting, 1988.

[9] The report of the consultation is *Fetters of Injustice*, ed. P. Gruber, Geneva, WCC, 1970.

[10] Konrad Raiser, in *Sharing Life: El Escorial Report*, ed. H. van Beek, Geneva, WCC, 1989, p.14.

[11] Minutes of the WCC Central Committee meeting, 1994, p.125.

[12] Darril Hudson, *The Ecumenical Movement in World Affairs*, London, Weidenfeld & Nicolson, 1969, p.150.

[13] *The Churches and the World Refugee Crisis*, Geneva, WCC, 1981, pp.14f.

[14] K. Poser, ed., *Called to be Neighbours: Larnaca Report*, Geneva, WCC, 1987, p.15.

[15] IDOC International Rome and CCPD reproduced the document with a bibliography in *Towards a Church in Solidarity with the Poor*, 1980.

[16] *Ecumenism and a New World Order*, Geneva, WCC, 1980, p.41.

[17] "The Economic Threat to Peace", *The Ecumenical Review*, vol. 27, no. 1, 1975, p.69.

2. "Not a Penny for the Missionaries": The Debate about Holism

The woman on the doorstep in north London raised a familiar issue. I was one of a quarter million churchgoers out on the streets collecting from door to door in what is known in the United Kingdom as Christian Aid Week. We visit almost every home in the country. We leave a red envelope and some information about Christian Aid's work. We ask for generous gifts for the poorest of the poor and we go back for the envelopes later in the week.

In the process, we get asked all sorts of questions. Sometimes we are drawn into argument, and while there are many cheerful givers, a few insist rather grimly on stating their terms. The name Christian Aid understandably makes people wonder whether we help only Christians, or whether we are really evangelists in aid-agency clothing, out to convert the heathen or win people of other faiths to the Christian cause. This particular woman was adamant that her money must not get mixed up with anything of that kind. She was ready to feed the hungry and help the poorest but "not a penny for the missionaries".

The issue she raised, though she would never have put it in these terms, was whether mission and development should be kept apart or held together. She was firmly of the opinion that they should be kept apart.

A Sudanese who once came to my doorstep took the opposite point of view. He came at night since, like Nicodemus, he had reason to be cautious of the authorities. During little more than a week in his country I had seen two pieces of work involving the Sudanese churches. One was among Eritrean refugees. They were anxious to go back home now that peace had come to their country after years of costly and courageous struggle. The other was among internal refugees displaced by Sudan's civil wars between North and South and within a South divided against itself.

The particular group of internal refugees I had visited had left their homes and fled North from the war some time earlier, along with 3 million others. They had tried to find shelter and eke out a living in the nooks and crannies of Khartoum, squatting on the patches of wasteland between its buildings. Now, for reasons best known to the city authorities, they were being forcibly removed to what looked to me to be a wilderness — flat, dusty and featureless sand — 15 kilometres outside of the city. On arrival, and I saw them coming, they were literally dumped — women, children, the elderly, a few sticks and plastic sheets, pots and pans — and left to fend for themselves. There were no services of any kind, and they had to dig holes to protect the old and the young from the cold night winds.

I thought that the churches with their overstretched resources would have more than enough to do trying to support such desperate people and meet their immediate needs. Nevertheless, there was something else on the mind of my night visitor. He lived in a country where there were not only issues of war. There were also issues of faith. He believed there was urgent work for the churches to do, not only reaching out to those in desperate need but also sharing and teaching the Christian faith under the eye of what was perceived to be a fundamentalist Islamic regime. He came to ask why agencies like mine seem so ready to help his church with its work among refugees and so unwilling to help when it comes to the work of evangelism. In his eyes we seem to agree with the woman in north London: "Not a penny for the missionaries". We seem to keep mission and development apart, whereas for him they belonged without question together.[1]

As a matter of fact, on that occasion we found a way of helping his church to produce some books and other materials for Christian education; but that in no way took the edge off the point he was making. It is a point which has been restated over and over again in the annals of the ecumenical response to poverty and human need over the past 50 years; so much so that it begins to take on the uninteresting if not unthoughtful sound of orthodoxy. In essence it advocates, indeed insists on, a rounded or "holistic" approach to the task of God's church and to the people God loves.

Holism: a chorus of approval

An early example is found in the WCC archives: the addresses by R.K. Orchard and W.A. Visser 't Hooft at a consultation organized by DICASR at Les Rasses, Switzerland, in 1956. Orchard insisted that

> the interrelation of *diakonia*, *apostole*, and *koinonia* [service, witness and fellowship] must be recognized and observed for the sake of the health and integrity of each of them. Thus *diakonia*, unless it is related to *apostole* can become merely a humanitarian service without anything distinctively Christian about it; and unless it is related to *koinonia* it can become an impersonal charity,... more concerned with the discharge of the giver's conscience than with real love for the recipient.

Visser 't Hooft was no less adamant

> that the service (*diakonia*) which the Christian churches are called to render to each other and to those outside the church who are in need of assistance is a fundamental aspect of the total mission of the Christian church, because it reflects the ministry of Christ himself... Inter-church aid must therefore always be conceived in its relationship to this total task and must never seek to compete with or even less to replace the missionary-evangelistic task.

Similar sentiments were expressed in terms of the eucharist at the CICARWS commission meeting in 1978:

> It is in the eucharistic act where we find the imperative for service in the world. The Lord whom we meet in the bread and wine is the same Lord whom we meet in the poor, the oppressed and the needy... Our Lord sends us to join him in bringing good news to the poor and the oppressed. [2]

Worship, communion, service and evangelism are all of a piece.

The WCC Faith and Order commission meeting in Lima in 1982 reflected the same sense of the eucharist as the focus of an all-embracing task:

> It is a representative act of thanksgiving and offering on behalf of the whole world. The eucharistic celebration demands reconciliation and sharing among all those regarded as brothers and sisters in the one family of God and is a constant challenge in the search for appropriate relationships in social, economic and political life. [3]

In 1978, at a consultation in Crete organized by CICARWS, Orthodox theologian Alexandros Papaderos put the doctrine of holism in a rather different way. His references to the "vertical" and "horizontal" speak of our relations with God and with each other:

> *In the context of the church's liturgical understanding of humanity, world, society and history, any division between verticalism and horizontalism is not merely absurd but actually heretical!*... Although we repudiate today the frequent misuse of diakonia as a means of proselytizing, it is impossible to detect any divorce between witness and service in the history of the church... Being the service of the whole human being and of the whole of humankind and of creation, diakonia involves a definite commitment to *social justice and liberation* yet at the same time respect for the divine commission to Christians to be messengers of *reconciliation* and sober insistence on the eschatological dimension of salvation.[4]

It comes as no surprise that CWME worked out its doctrine of holism in terms of a "comprehensive understanding of salvation" at a world conference in Bangkok in 1973.[5] Equally unsurprisingly, CICARWS worked it out in terms of "service" or diakonia, notably at its world consultation in Larnaca in 1986:

> Diakonia is seen as a part of the global mission of the church: koinonia, diakonia, kerygma and martyria [that is, fellowship, service, preaching and witness] belonging together... Diakonia is service to the whole of the human being, to all of humanity and to the whole of creation and means engagement for reconciliation, social justice and liberation.

Klaus Poser, then director of CICARWS, declared that

> diakonia is comprehensive. Too long has it been identified with the charitable service of the church only... Being an expression of faith, diakonia is also holistic; service cannot be separated from witness, it cannot be separated from obedience, and from the eucharist. Any separation leads to alienation and brokenness. Diakonia appeals to and involves the whole church, with all its charisma.

An African working group at the same consultation agreed:

> The diaconal work of the church should be comprehensive. It encompasses the total ministry and life of the church. It is liberating and invigorating. And it is concerned with both the spiritual and material conditions of all God's people including the youth, women and the laity.[6]

While the principal concern of the world consultation in El Escorial, Spain, in 1987, was to find more acceptable ways of sharing resources between the churches of North and South, questions about the task for which those resources were to be used could hardly be avoided. The answer was the holistic mission of the church. The published report of the consultation in fact includes a section on "Wholeness", which calls on the churches not to separate the spiritual, human, cultural and material dimensions of life:

> The ecumenical sharing of resources cannot function with a division between the spiritual and the material... All the activities of the Christian community in evangelism, diakonia, the struggle for human dignity, healing, peace and justice belong together in the one mission of God.

In drawing up "Guidelines for Sharing" the participants committed themselves, among other things,

> to promote through words and deeds the holistic mission of the church in obedience to God's liberating will. We are convinced that in responding only to certain parts of the mission we distort and disrupt mission as a whole.[7]

Holism thus wins a chorus of approval. Like "inclusive", however, "holistic" is an elastic term easily stretched to cover a range of meanings. Service for example can be holistic or inclusive because it serves everyone irrespective of creed. It can be holistic because it is the work of the whole church, from local congregations to specialist agencies, making good use of its many and varied gifts and skills; or because it is offered in many different ways, from the highly personal and face-to-face to the political and the more indirect benefits of structural change. Service can also be holistic because it accepts that there is a greater whole, like the total mission of the church, of which it is only a part; or because it has a certain comprehensiveness within itself, recognizing for example that if you are really going to serve the community's best interests you will almost certainly need to foster good relationships among its people just as much as you will need to develop a more sustainable economy.

The main focus of interest however is to hold together the material and the spiritual, the needs of the body, mind and soul, mission (or more precisely evangelism) and development. And the perpetual insistence in ecumenical documents that this is how it ought to be suggests that this has not always been the case, that this rounded approach to the task of the church has in practice if not in theory been in danger of being denied or ignored.

Together or apart?

A careful look at the evidence does not altogether bear this out, especially in the earlier years. For example, the missionary movements that came together in the IMC had long had aspirations to holistic mission, with schools and medical work and artisan missionaries alongside preaching and teaching. William Carey, the Baptist pioneer, asked for seeds with which to develop agricultural work in Bengal as early as the 19th century.[8] Other missionaries were organizing relief work in China.[9] Eugene Carson Blake, then general secretary of the WCC, spoke of the involvement of missionaries in development at an ecumenical consultation in Montreux, Switzerland, in 1970:

> The churches, through their missionary movements, have a long and impressive record of involvement in service and development projects. Service has been a major feature of Christian mission in developing countries since the late nineteenth century.[10]

Furthermore, missionaries and their experiences in the mission field did much to energize the ecumenical movement, and when the WCC formally came into being with departments responsible for aid and development work, good cooperation between the Council and the missionary movement continued. There was no apparent falling apart.

As we have seen, the Commission of the Churches on International Affairs (CCIA) was founded in 1946 as a common enterprise of the WCC and the IMC. So was a committee for Refugee Relief in the Near East set up in 1951. Cooperation is clearly reflected in a joint statement by the IMC and WCC in May 1953 that DICASR should "act for both bodies in relation to the co-ordination and ecumenical presentation of emergency inter-church aid and relief needs in all countries outside Europe in which both the IMC and WCC have interests and responsibilities." Non-emergency work was also to be a matter for consultation and cooperation.

When the WCC's Evanston assembly in 1954 gave DICASR a full mandate to work in Africa, Asia and Latin America, it became urgent to agree with the missionary movements and already well established churches there how best this could be done. An attempt was made at a meeting in St Albans, England, to draw up a sensible and acceptable division of labour within the overall task. The agreement, contained in a statement on "Mission and Service: Their Theological Unity and Its Consequences", became known a year later as the Herrenalb Categories (after the place in Germany where the joint committee on inter-church aid and mission met). Though never officially adopted, these remained in force until 1965. The agreement confined inter-church aid to emergency situations, to the needs of refugees, to churches without missionary support and to work which missionary agencies were unable to support.

Cooperation apparently grew stronger in 1964 when the categories were made less distinct, and inter-church aid (now DICARWS) was allowed to help churches supported by missionary agencies through its project list. Even after the Herrenalb Categories were abolished in 1965 by the WCC central committee, new agreements were made. In 1966, the WCC's Division of World Mission and Evangelism (DWME) became responsible for longer-term programmes and DICARWS for projects usually expected to become self-supporting within five years;[11] and the two divisions shared a joint project list which allowed both service and evangelization to find a place.[12]

Despite these practical attempts to hold the ecumenical work of the churches together, there is evidence that it was indeed falling apart. In 1974 the Lutheran World Federation held a consultation in Nairobi on "Proclamation and Human Development". It was apparently provoked by a letter to the Federation from the Mekane Yesu Church in Ethiopia. The church's concern was exactly the same as that of the Sudanese Christian who came to visit me that evening in Khartoum. It was being challenged by enormous human needs — Ethiopia would before long be inseparably associated in the Western mind with famine, drought and death — and yet the task of proclaiming the gospel and touching and turning the inner life of the people to Christ could not be ignored. It was not however being supported. There was no longer a balance between aid for proclamation and aid for development. More money was available for the latter. The letter appealed to the agencies on their own terms, challenging their concept of development and suggesting that aid should be made available for evangelistic purposes because, in the church's opinion, development of the inner person is a prerequisite for healthy and lasting human development overall.

By the time of the two world consultations in Larnaca (1986) and El Escorial (1987), the separation of mission and development was being referred to openly not as a risk to be avoided but an unfortunate reality to be overcome. Konrad Raiser in his opening address at El Escorial confessed that "we have been talking about the wholeness of the church's mission in witness and service in all six continents for a long time now. But mission and development continue as before to be separate fields." [13] El Escorial's effort to put matters right was not very successful, and the situation remains much the same.

The terms of the debate

When it comes to asking why the separation of mission and development persists despite the constant reaffirmation of holism, and what if anything should be done about it, the documented voices of the ecumenical movement are fairly silent. There is silence too at the level of theology, especially within the historic stream of Life and Work, in which DICARWS, CICARWS and now Unit IV stand. Little analysis or critical and constructive thinking that might underpin a more satisfactory way forward is to be found. So it is difficult to record much of a debate; we can only try instead to set out some of its terms. There are at least seven. Two have to do with the origins of the division between mission and development in (1) disenchantment with missionaries and (2) the growth of specialized agencies. The next three can be seen as ways of healing or at least alleviating the harmful effects of the division by (3) retreating from both mission and development, (4) creating more holistic agencies or (5) agreeing to a division of labour within the whole. The final two ask whether the division is between different parts of the whole or is due to (6) inadequate or (7) different holistic understandings of the church's task.

1. Disenchantment with missionaries

The historic missionary movement from North to South at one time had seemed heroic, inspiring and at the heart of the church's task in the world. The reasons why this changed during the second half of the 20th century are well known. In so far as overseas missions could be identified with colonialism and the spread of empire, doubts about the one easily rubbed off onto the other and contributed to the demise of both. These doubts had to do with the vested interests and exploitative nature of such movements. They set out to do others good, bringing them culture, civilization and the blessings of the gospel; but too often it seemed that most of the benefits were enjoyed, if not by the heroic pioneers themselves, then certainly by the countries from which they came. There seemed to be little respect for the rights and cultures or the long-term well-being of the people to whom they were sent.

Besides growing doubts about missionary movements, there were doubts about Christianity itself. The rising tide of science, with its thirst for evidence, and of secularism and pluralism sapped its confidence. The Christian religion and its institutional expression in the churches became more marginal in national affairs and international relations. The basis for its interventions and influence seemed much more fragile, and the reasons why the Christian faith should be pressed upon peoples of other faiths as the supreme truth and the one real hope of their salvation were far less obvious. Christianity began to look like one view of truth among many, and for many people it was not in fact a very convincing one. Surely it should try to interact in modest and respectful ways with other views of truth and other religions rather than attempt to lord it over them. Surely its claims were relative rather than absolute, and its advocates should conduct themselves accordingly.

In any case, Christianity was no longer the preserve of the churches in Europe or the North — not that, taking a broader view of the history of the church, it ever had been. With the end of empires and the growing independence, at least in formal political terms, of the nations of the South, there was an increasing awareness that the so-called "younger churches" were no longer content to be dominated, shaped and coloured by the mission agencies and mission boards of the sending churches, but insisted on taking on a life of their own. This independence made missionary activities as traditionally understood seem inappropriate. It was for the younger churches to carry out their own missions in their own way. More than that, mission had to be a two-way affair, in which the South equally contributed its insights and energies to the task of re-evangelizing the dispirited churches and communities of the North. Mutuality and partnership in mission, where gifts and resources were shared and all were givers and receivers, seemed far better ways of approaching the church's task across the world.

Even if some of the criticisms of missionaries were crude and unjust, this is how they came to be perceived. In the eyes of the woman on the doorstep with whom we began this chapter, they were closed-minded absolutists, winning people to their cause and disrespectful of other religions, thus doing more harm than good. No matter if she herself was equally closed-minded. Missionaries were against the spirit of the age. History was passing them by. They were no longer exciting but anachronistic. Other movements looked much more appropriate and promising, not least the movement for world development.

Ironically this movement, which came into its own after the second world war and of which the church development agencies and DICARWS and CICARWS came to be a part, is open at many points to the same kind of criticisms, hesitations and doubts that surrounded the missionaries, although this was not immediately recognized. In 1973, for example, the Council of the Evangelical Church in Germany (EKD) declared that

> the ties between the missionary movement and colonial imperialism have in some developing countries produced such misgiving in respect to missions that only development programmes and ecumenical forms of service remain as possible forms of Christian presence. [14]

In fact, development programmes were in many ways just as disrespectful, if not more so, of other cultures and ways of seeing things, insisting that the North and the rich knew best. Like the missionaries, they were peddlers of a faith and in many cases of an absolutist kind of faith in a particular economic programme which they believed would rescue millions of people from poverty. They too went to the South in the guise of doing good and often ended up as the midwives of exploitation. And they were often less successful than the missionaries at recognizing the rights of others to their independence and fostering it, trapping poor countries in new spirals of dependency, as the trading patterns of the world and the international debt crisis still show. If the fight against poverty seemed more in tune with the spirit of the age (and disenchantment may now be setting in there as well), it was no less open to criticism and often on much the same grounds.

Nevertheless, however unclear or facile the reasons, enthusiasm and sympathy for missionaries and missionary societies and agencies largely died. They lost the support, not only of those who were now outside the churches, but of those who remained inside as well. In part this may have been because their constituency had shrunk and there was less money to be had in any case, but it was also because the interest and allegiance of churchgoers seemed to shift elsewhere. The churches of the South which still looked to the missionary societies for the funds to support their holistic enterprises, especially those aspects which the better-off development agencies were not prepared or able to fund, discovered that the missionary societies, no matter how willing they might have been, were no longer able to respond.

2. Specialized agencies

The second origin of the growing divide between mission and development lies in the increasing number of specialized development agencies following the second world war. As the churches rose to the challenge of refugees and reconstruction in Europe and then of poverty across all six continents, the agencies were the instruments of their response. The charge that they were responsible for the divide is reflected in some of the ecumenical documents referred to earlier. Take for example the words of Alexandros Papaderos at Larnaca in 1986:

> We do not need an independent official diaconal bureaucracy, but a truly liturgical diakonia, which has its source of power in the holy eucharist as all-encompassing love, as dispenser of life and hope! [15]

Another interpretation of Larnaca puts it this way:

> Today the churches of the South are... questioning the donor-receiver relationship not just because it is a one-way street, but also because it is seen as a technical relationship on the part of the Western agencies. It is a relationship deprived of wholeness, reduced to the transfer of money and the inspection of projects and accounts... Relationships must be holistic; they must encompass the whole life of the churches and not get hung up on reporting and agency criteria. [16]

The report from El Escorial also implied that a significant reason why mission and development fell apart was to be found in the corresponding institutions and structures which often operated separately and therefore needed to be transformed and changed. There was a need "to work out new mechanisms bringing the two together". [17]

Already in 1978, the CWME executive committee had distanced itself from the agencies in setting out its own particular interests:

> 1. CWME's interest lies in the promotion of relationships in mission, not of technical relationships of service, although they have their own legitimacy.
>
> 2. We are interested in the promotion of an holistic approach to mission; we are not interested in social service per se, nor are we interested in relationships with governments or independent funding agencies.

What made these ecumenical agencies a threat to "holism"? In the first place, their ecumenical virtue could become a vice. In earlier ecumenical days it was often claimed that "doctrine divides and service unites". In other words, while it is very difficult for the churches to agree on what they believe, above all about the church, ministry and sacraments (Faith and Order), it is relatively easy for them to get on and do things together (Life and Work). Time would show that this is not always the case, but it is certainly true that some of the pioneering ecumenical achievements were in the realms of practical service, and the aid and development agencies were — and in some countries still are — outstanding examples.

Their achievement in being ecumenical however carried with it the risk that instead of drawing the churches together into common life and witness, ecumenical endeavours, including councils of churches and agencies, can loosen their ties with the churches (as can the churches with them), thus developing a life of their own. Rather than identifying with the churches, ecumenical institutions have a tendency to go their own way. The churches see these institutions as something other than, if not over against, themselves. This can make it more difficult for an agency to maintain a churchly character and easier for it to pursue its own agenda. Holism seems to be peculiarly at risk in all of this, since in many ways it speaks of the essential elements of the church's task, of which the church is the guardian and true expression, not least in its congregational life. To be detached from the churches, as ecumenical bodies and agencies — much more than missionary societies — are prone to be, is to run the risk of being detached from their essentially rounded character.

Second, holism may be threatened because development agencies have become specialized. This is partly because development has come to be seen as something of a professional discipline. It is studied in university departments and institutes. It is the subject of research. It has its schools of thought. It requires technical skills in agriculture, water engineering, health care, education and so on. It needs the subtler skills of community workers and organizers. It must handle the inter-related fields of micro- and macro-economics. It is not for amateurs, however intelligent, thus separating it on a second count from ordinary people in local congregations and their holistic calling. As Klaus Poser remarked at Larnaca in 1986: "We have the institutionalization and professionalization of diakonia. Have these reduced the ability of people to interact and to serve?"[18]

The drive towards specializing is also the result of a desire to be efficient and effective. The job must be done well, and if you are to do it well, you must not only be competent, but also acknowledge that you cannot be competent in everything. By definition, to specialize is to concentrate on the part and not the whole. You narrow your sights; and in doing so there is an in-built threat to holism.

Third, the same tendency to be selective arises from the mandates given to agencies either formally by the churches which create them or in an unwritten form by what their supporters and backers expect them to do. Many of them were created precisely to meet immediate human need and to help poor communities overcome material poverty, not to do evangelism or Christian education. And many are not expected to range beyond what holistic theology might regard as an over-narrow brief, either into politics on the one hand or into overtly sharing the Christian faith on the other. They would lose their donors if they did.

Increasingly, these donors have not been confined to churches and the public but include governments as well. Agencies may try to make sure they are not mere handmaidens of government policies; but governments are bound to lay down conditions and to have their own strong ideas as to what agencies should and should not do.

Thus when the Sudanese Christian mentioned earlier came to me by night gently criticizing the aid agencies for helping the refugees in his country but not the work of promoting the Christian faith, I had to confront him with a hard choice. Those who provided the money he wanted to use did not give it to be spent on missionary work, however valid or important both of us might regard it; and if they saw it being used in that way their giving would stop. He either had to accept money for limited purposes or face the prospect of having no money at all.

There is a fourth reason why ecumenical agencies can pose a threat to holism. The agencies, especially in the earlier part of their history, can be seen as working almost entirely among or within the churches. The phrase "inter-church aid" suggests precisely that. It was a brave departure, since each church was being challenged not simply to look after its own but to see itself as part of a wider family in which all would be enabled to fulfil their calling, whether large or small, whether of the same tradition or another. [19] Many rose to that challenge. But it was an internal affair. It was inter-church and intra-church, even if it benefited many beyond the church.

In time, however, the church's involvement in development through its specialized agencies became an example of a familiar phenomenon in Christian history: the movement of Christians out of the church and into the common life of the world to contribute to its endeavours and to shape its life for the better — ideally according to the pattern of God's kingdom. This movement brings Christian men and women into business and commerce, social work, politics, charities, schools, medicine, the arts and many other spheres of life, not only to earn a living and do the world's work, but to help to redeem and transform it. The work of Christian aid agencies, not just within and between the churches but also alongside other so-called secular agencies (they would certainly not wish to identify themselves as Christian or religious, even though many have deep moral and spiritual roots), governments and other development institutions, is one more example.

This movement seemed to be approved by the WCC executive committee in 1970 when it encouraged CCPD (the Commission on the Churches' Participation in Development) to develop relationships not only with churches but also with governments, voluntary agencies, other faiths and secular movements.

Being part of such a movement involves accepting that you cannot simply pursue your goals on your own terms. [20] To require an holistic approach, combining mission and development at every step, might be regarded as doing just that. Some will see settling for less as a compromise, even a betrayal of Christian principles. Others will see it as serving a higher principle and a wider ecumenism. The world in which human beings have to live together is grossly unjust and unhappy. We hold very different views and are unlikely ever to hold the same. Amidst our diversity and disagreement we have to search for common ground on which to build a common life. The cost of doing so in terms of being true to our faith may at times be too high and we have to draw back. There will always be a healthy critical tension; but more often than not we shall see the wisdom of restraint and of going forward, perhaps not on our own ideal terms but on good terms with those of other faiths and of none. We shall not therefore always see self-denial over evangelism or some other aspect of a rounded view of Christian mission — in which those outside the church cannot share — as a failure to do what Christians ought to do, but as part of the reality of doing what Christians are positively called to do, namely to build our world with all women and men of good will. We see this point quite clearly in many spheres. We do not expect politicians or social workers to be evangelists, partly because we respect the specialist nature of their work but also because we understand the more broadly based, co-operative nature of what they are about in a pluralist world. The same should be true of aid and development.

Of course that begs the question as to whether it is done by aid and development agencies carrying a Christian label rather than by individuals who make their Christian contribution within secular agencies alongside and in dialogue with everybody else. This debate is similar to the one about Christians in politics and Christian political parties. The engagement may be highly desirable but is a corporate Christian identity any longer appropriate or necessary? Do we need for example a "Christian Aid" as well as an "Oxfam" in order for Christians to be true to their extramural responsibilities to development?

Thus mission and development may well have been separated by the rise of specialized development agencies. The outcome should be regretted above all if it signals an inadequate response to human need. But it might be understood and accepted, even positively welcomed, as one way in which Christians become actively involved with others in constructing a different kind of world. In that case, this second possible reason for the separation of mission and development also contains within it a suggested response to the problem. The next three aspects of the debate suggest three more.

3. The retreat from both mission and development

We have seen that many of the criticisms levelled at the overseas missionary movement apply with equal force to the world development movement. Both have imperial tendencies; both impose on people instead of respecting their right to decide for themselves. As a result, the primary locus of concern about Western churches and agencies in their dealings with the Third World should not be that they contribute to a divorce between mission and development, but that they are involved in them at all. It is for poorer people as well as the materially better-off to decide for themselves what development means for them and what they are going to believe and what adds up to a better quality of life. It is not for others to decide on their behalf. The responsibility of those who wish to offer support to the poor is to make it possible for the poor to take decisions that actually make a difference.

To make the point in another way, when Western agencies are criticized for funding one part of an holistic task and not another, the proper response may be not to fund both but in a sense to fund neither. They should not see themselves as involved in either mission or development but as helping to create the conditions for both. Their task is a kind of preparation for mission and development, making it possible for those to whom these tasks properly belong to carry them out on their own terms.

There are hints at such an understanding in some of the statements surrounding the so-called Herrenalb Categories, which took the holistic approach very seriously. For example, a July 1966 document spoke of the common concern of DWME and DICASR "to express the ecumenical solidarity of the churches through material aid to strengthen them in their life and mission". [21]

This conviction obviously relates to discussions about power to which we must come later, but it raises three questions we should register now.

First, what kind of supportive activities do you get involved in if you are determined to create the conditions for mission and development without actually carrying them out yourself? Two of the most obvious contemporary answers would be: the more equal sharing of the world's resources, without which it is well-nigh impossible for anyone to have much of a life, and the maximizing of people's freedom to choose for themselves and decide what happens to them. These are the pre-conditions, and these are the legitimate business of the outsider. The WCC assembly in Canberra in 1991 seemed to agree when it reaffirmed the Guidelines for Sharing from El Escorial and described the ecumenical sharing of resources not only as a way of bringing mission and service together but also as a means of "committing ourselves as churches to the sharing of power and resources so that all may fully participate in mission". [22]

Second, how can one work in practice with any notion of a chronological sequence in which the necessary conditions are first created and then mission and development proceed apace? Are all these processes not inter-related, and will the later ones not always refuse to wait on the earlier? Is it not entirely unrealistic to imagine that we can in any sense move a step at a time, or in this case lay the foundations before erecting the building?

And third, granted that one of the deepest suspicions of the missionary and development movements is that they illegitimately impose values on people who must be free to decide for themselves, are not the so-called pre-conditions we are invited to help create equally value-laden and full of assumptions about what is good for other people and what is not? "Democracy", for example, can be a useful shorthand way of referring to the rights of people to choose for themselves what they wish to believe and how they are going to live. But "democracy" is not a neutral term, and it is often used to export the assumptions of one culture to another.

Thus the proposal of stepping back from both mission and development to help create the conditions for both is not without its own complexities. But it may suggest where the emphasis should lie, and may well provide fruitful common ground with people of other faiths.

4. Holistic agencies

A second, quite different response to the divorce between mission and development is to create and sustain holistic agencies which confidently address themselves to a wide-ranging, holistic task. Many of the missionary societies upheld just such an ideal, setting up hospitals, running schools and working on agricultural projects as well as doing the work of evangelism and forming churches.

An organization like Tearfund in the UK offers a more recent example. It is itself the fruit of an attempt by evangelicals to recover the more rounded approach to the church's task which they once had in abundance but lost. It has now been restored, not by adding evangelism to development but by recognizing the claims of social responsibility and social justice (of which development is a part) alongside those of preaching the gospel and winning people to faith in Christ. The recovery is embodied in an agency which calls itself a missionary society or movement but is clearly committed to the struggle against poverty.

Such a bold and rounded approach raises a number of issues. One already referred to is the difficulty of getting this relationship right. Our intentions can all too easily be misunderstood. Evangelicals and others will no doubt insist that the offer of food, health care or education and the offer of the good news of salvation are equally offers of love, reflecting the genuine concern of God and God's servants for the good of the poor. Indeed, one without the other would be a totally inadequate reflection of that love and concern. Everything that is done is equally disinterested Christian service. But it has not always looked that way from the outside. Holistic enterprises have often looked more like sectarian crusades, competing with other forms of Christianity, dividing communities (between Protestant and Catholic, Protestant and Protestant, Christian and Muslim, etc.) and recruiting people to particular causes in which political interests seem as much to the fore as humanitarian and evangelical ones.

Even where this is not true, it is easily suspected as being true. Those who come bearing gifts have hidden agendas, so beware. They are really coming to proselytize, not because they care for the people but because they are looking out for their own cause. Under such circumstances, the response of the recipients can then be both astute and cynical. They become "rice Christians", seeming to accept the faith in order to gain access to the practical help they really value.

The examples are by no means confined to the world of evangelicals. In the 1960s and 1970s the base Christian communities, especially in Latin America, were much admired and emulated as examples of holism. The Bible and the issues of everyday life were put firmly together. Justice for the poor was intrinsically related to the mission of Jesus who came to announce good news to them. Daily bread and the bread of life were all of a piece. But in recent years, as some of the worst of Latin America's dictatorships have crumbled and opportunities for political activity have opened up, there has been an exodus from the base communities. Many have left to join political movements outside the church. The suspicion arises — and even if it is true it is not necessarily a criticism — that the base communities were attractive not primarily because of the Christian faith they offered and professed, however enlightened and progressive it may have been, but because of the space and opportunity they provided for debate and action on social and political issues which was denied to people everywhere else. If some were inspired by Christian faith to political obedience, others were "rice Christians", apparently accepting the faith in order to gain access to the limited political opportunities they really valued.

The relationship between mission and development is thus difficult to get right when it comes to practical service on the ground. It is also quite difficult to see where an agency's task begins or ends once it is committed to an holistic programme. The argument is for a comprehensive approach to the church's task and a comprehensive response to human need. But all of this cannot be summed up in the two words "mission" and "development". We have to add other words as well: "worship", "teaching", "service", "prophecy", "pastoral care". How far are agencies of the church, committed to holism, required to go?

Logic appears to lead in two directions. One is towards being a church or a para-church. This is a very real temptation for movements which become impatient with the churches' response to poverty and long to evoke and sustain in Christian people a more adequate way of being with the poor of the earth, which includes not only their giving but their worship and life-style. In the past missionary movements have in effect been churches on the move from one part of the world to another; but I doubt that it is the intention or destiny of aid and development agencies to do the same.

The logic of a thoroughgoing commitment to holism could lead in another direction. The agency itself would not get directly involved; rather, it would openly resource and fund the church of the poor across the whole spectrum of its activities without any hesitation or "earmarking" — which is not the way aid agencies normally behave. Once again this raises issues of power. For example, on what conditions would the resources be shared? And it would jeopardize any funding from outside the church. But it does look more like a respectful retreat from both mission and development and many other aspects of another church's work to being content instead to prepare the ground or to create and sustain the possibility for them all. Holistic agencies do not appear to follow either logic very systematically.

5. A division of labour

What might be called a commonsense reaction to the issues raised by the perceived divorce between mission and development is to hold that within the holistic task a sensible division of labour is required, in which no agency claims to have or is criticized for having anything but a limited agenda. This approach was clearly adopted in the 1950s with the Herrenalb Categories.

Such an approach fully acknowledges that there is an holistic task to be done in response to poverty and encourages the churches, locally, regionally or globally, to rise to this task. It accepts that certain agencies can have a specific role to play without necessarily having to try to do everything, while insisting that all agencies keep the wider, more comprehensive vision clearly in view and see that their individual and separate contributions are constantly related to it. The holistic framework within which this sensible division of labour takes place can be generated from without or from within, and preferably from both.

One example "from without" is the concept of the round table, steadily developed and reviewed by the ecumenical family over the years. Originally it brought together around one table representatives of a national council of churches in a Third World country, the WCC and Northern funding agencies. The holistic framework was generated by the council of churches as it set out its total programme, including evangelism, Christian education, relief and development. The funding agencies supported different aspects of the programme according to their various mandates; and together there was some possibility of funding the whole. The concept of "partnership in mission" coming out of the missionary movement is in many ways similar to the round table.

Round tables, like all institutions, have their limitations. They have tended to talk too much about money and too little about the holistic task. They have focused too narrowly on the programmes and interests of the councils of churches and insufficiently on the churches themselves, which the councils exist to represent and draw together in a common ecumenical enterprise. And where holistic programmes have emerged, some aspects of them have been far better supported than others. But there are possibilities for improvement. More adequate forums might be developed, in which the churches and other sympathetic partners within a country or region would have a better opportunity to develop a shared understanding of and a more adequate and comprehensive response to poverty, embracing the spiritual and intellectual challenges it presents as warmly as the practical and material ones. Ecumenical councils can also improve their ability to listen to and represent the views of local churches where the church's holistic task must finally be rooted and carried forward. What do these churches have to do and what then needs to be advocated in their name? Again, those invited and prepared to accompany the churches in their work can see to it that there is a wider range of agencies represented around the table: relief and development agencies, missionary societies, solidarity movements, confessional bodies, organizations mandated to feed the minds as well as feed the hungry; so that there is a better chance that among them wide-ranging support can be given. Some agencies might be of even more help if they were to target their contributions in a rather more focused way than their own aspirations to holism might otherwise tempt them to do. For example, mission agencies, which alone can offer funds for Christian education and evangelism, might eschew support for agricultural or medical work if that can be more easily funded from elsewhere.

But an holistic framework, within which a division of labour then looks like common sense, must not be generated only from without. It must also be generated from within. An agency or organization which does not claim to be comprehensive in the work it tries to do must nevertheless look for a certain kind of wholeness for itself by fashioning its own comprehensive understanding of the church's task in bringing good news to the poor and understanding just as clearly where and how its own contribution fits in. It must constantly test and inform and re-adjust the part it plays in relation to its understanding of the whole. Here is one of the points at which it must do theology.

This brings us to two final and perhaps more fundamental aspects of the debate about mission and development.

6. Inadequate frameworks

What has often contributed to the divide between mission and development are inadequate frameworks of understanding which have made agencies dismissive of some aspects of the church's response to poverty, not just because they were outside their remit but because they were regarded as unimportant. The most obvious example of this is the inadequate concepts of development which have been allowed to set the parameters within which aid and development agencies all too often set about their work, accepting the conventional wisdom and confining themselves to narrow economic and technical concepts. Complementary emphases on culture and civil society are now becoming more accepted. These allow for a more sympathetic appreciation of the promotion of values, religious practices and organizations and for the building up of church institutions as being of value in their own right and not merely according to their potential as instruments of material progress. As a result development agencies may be "allowed" to fund where they said they could not fund before.

7. Different holistic frameworks

Finally, the rift between mission and development may have its roots not in the drifting apart of two different aspects of a single whole, but in fundamentally different understandings of that whole. Deep disagreements between different holistic theologies lead some to go much further than merely opting for one task rather than another within a sensible division of labour. They actually reject one task in favour of another. They choose development or mission, because it is more compatible with their understanding of what the totality of the church's business in the world is all about.

To conjure up a sense of those deeper differences we need only to remind ourselves of the claims of "universal" (Western) theology against those of contextual theology, or contrast conservative evangelical theology with liberation theology. We might also illustrate them with two caricatures, unlike the real world but not unrelated to it. One takes as its cue what might be called the "organizing principle" of the gospel for the sinner; the other, the gospel for the poor.

Where "good news for the sinner" is seen as the core of the church's task and the organizing principle of the holistic view of mission, several consequences will follow. First, there will be little to choose between any human beings as to which of them should hear the gospel before all others. All have sinned and come short of the glory of God. All are called to repent and receive God's forgiveness. Rich and poor are on the same level of spiritual need. There is no particular reason for singling out the materially deprived or socially excluded, any more than there is for ignoring the better-off. Second, the key tasks of the church would tend to be vocal and verbal. The good news is essentially a message that can be announced, a gospel that can be preached, a story that can be told. Its truth can be heard and its benefits enjoyed without any change in concrete circumstances. The gospel may be about the incarnate Word but it is no longer essentially incarnate. Sinners can simply be told about God's love in Christ. Third, while the importance of addressing the basic needs of desperate people, giving them food and clothing, dressing their wounds and visiting them in prison, would never be denied, it is not intrinsic to salvation. It is an outworking of Christian kindness which follows on after what matters most, rather than being essentially a part of it.

Where "good news for the poor" is seen as the core and the organizing principle, different consequences will follow. First, it is quite clear that the poor have a prior claim on the church's attention. The gospel is not about forgiving sins so much as about overcoming hunger and injustice, putting the last and the least first and lifting the burdens of oppression. This sets clear priorities as to which people you bother about first. There is a defined, prime target audience. Second, the key tasks of the church will tend to be active and practical. The gospel is essentially embodied or incarnate. What Christians have to say may from time to time explain how they are inspired to do what they do. It will shine through and deeds will become luminous, but it is the doing which is essential; whereas for those who preach the gospel of God's forgiveness, loving deeds may go to prove that all the talk of love is not sheer hypocrisy but they are not the substance of the gospel itself. Third, the concern about poverty is not an *implication* of the gospel as it is worked out in the life of the believer. It is the *definition* of the gospel: the point at which everything Christian has to begin.

It is interesting and important to note that it is the missionary wing of the ecumenical movement, rather than its aid and development arm, which has come closest to articulating this second holistic view when in Melbourne in 1980 the WCC's world mission conference affirmed the proclamation of the gospel for and especially by the poor as an essential task of the church. The churches are urged to become "churches in solidarity with the struggles of the poor", "to participate in the struggle themselves", to become "churches of the poor". [23] This call is also heard in the CCPD study of the church and the poor (see chapter 5).

One might extend this crude typology of "good news for the sinner" and "good news for the poor" to suggest how these different organizing principles lead to differing emphases on the church as an institution and differing attitudes to other faiths; but perhaps what has been said is enough to illustrate that our story may not simply be one of a single whole tending to fall apart, but of different holisms which tend to find the world of mission or the world of development more congenial. One response to this is to attempt to fuse these differing holisms into one at a more interesting and inspiring and more honest level than simply saying that evangelism and development deserve equal emphasis and that a proper balance should be struck, since both have an essential contribution to make. Another response is to accept the pluralism of different forms of Christianity with their different holisms and organizing principles and learn how to live with it creatively in an ecumenical community of disagreement.

In summary, the ecumenical family in responding to poverty appears to have been strongly in favour of an holistic approach to the life and work of the church and in particular to mission and development, and has voiced its loud regrets when it appeared to be falling apart. It has been less diligent in searching for more satisfactory theologies which might hold different emphases together, and less successful in finding ways of enabling Christian organizations, with their differing and partial contributions, to work together more effectively. Beyond that it may still have to face the fact that at bottom we are dealing not with a division of labour but with deep divisions of opinion about the nature of the gospel.

In 1983 the WCC's Vancouver assembly decided that growth towards "vital and coherent theology" should be one of the priorities of all the programmes of the WCC. An advisory group was to be formed to foster it. [24]

The word "coherent" suggests an exercise in convergence, reconciling all the various parts into an adequate whole: evangelism and social action, salvation history and human history, mission and development, vertical and horizontal, preaching and practice, prayer and politics, ideas and actions, classic and contextual. [25] The word "vital" sounds more creative. It suggests not just the sum of the parts but a lively and fresh holistic theology beyond the now familiar and fading ones of the West and the South. Like all others it would run the risk of not pleasing everyone and so continuing the debate not between different parts of the whole but different holistic theologies.

Recalling the mandate regarding vital and coherent theology, the moderator of the WCC central committee told the Canberra assembly in 1991 that "the task we were set still remains ahead of us". [26] If a theological task remains, so does an institutional one. Not only do we still have mission and development agencies which relate to each other and their churches with difficulty, but we also still have agencies in the North with specialized agendas ill-matched with councils of churches in the South with holistic agendas: the continuing expression of the age-old debate.

NOTES

[1] See *A Growing Partnership*, Board of Mission of the General Synod of the Church of England, 1994, p.10, para. 45.
[2] "Service and Unity", *Midstream*, Vol. 28, 1979, pp.174f.
[3] *Baptism, Eucharist and Ministry*, Faith and Order Paper 111, Geneva, WCC, 1982, p.14.
[4] *An Orthodox Approach to Diaconia*, Geneva, WCC, 1980, pp.23, 28, 42.
[5] Minutes of the Bangkok assembly, p.89.
[6] *The Larnaca Digest*, Geneva, WCC, 1987, pp.2f.; *Called to be Neighbours*, pp.82, 105.
[7] *Sharing Life*, pp.43, 45, 29.
[8] Cf. W. Schot, *Do We Project Ourselves in Projects?*, Geneva, WCC, 1977, p.13.
[9] See T. Early, *Simply Sharing*, Geneva, WCC, 1980, p.31.

[10] *Fetters of Injustice*, p.20.

[11] See G. Murray, in *A History of the Ecumenical Movement*, Vol. 2, pp.217f.

[12] Minutes of the Bangkok assembly, pp.14f.; Digest of the Swanwick consultation, 1966, p.121.

[13] *Sharing Life*, pp.15f.

[14] "The Church's Service to Development", *The Ecumenical Review*, Vol. 26, 1974, p.119.

[15] *Called to be Neighbours*, p.61.

[16] C. Ceccon and K. Paludan, eds, *My Neighbour — Myself*, Geneva, WCC, 1988, pp.29f.

[17] *Sharing Life*, p.40.

[18] *Called to be Neighbours*, p.83.

[19] See *The Ten Formative Years: Report to the Amsterdam Assembly*, Geneva, WCC, 1948, p.33.

[20] See K. van der Poort, "Resource Sharing and Project Funding", *The Ecumenical Review*, Vol. 38, 1986, p.432.

[21] See G. Murray in *History of the Ecumenical Movement*, Vol. 2, p.218.

[22] M. Kinnamon, ed., *Signs of the Spirit*, p.102.

[23] *Your Kingdom Come*, Geneva, WCC, 1980, p.177.

[24] D. Gill, ed., *Gathered for Life*, Geneva, WCC, 1983, pp.253f.

[25] This variety was a major issue of contention at the Nairobi assembly; cf. Paton, *Breaking Barriers*, p.30; and R. Dickinson, in *To Set at Liberty the Oppressed*, Geneva, WCC, 1975, pp.41f., and 98f.

[26] *Signs of the Spirit*, p.25.

3. "Keep Politics Out of It": The Debate about Structural Change

The story of the ecumenical response to poverty is very largely a story about the funding of "projects". They are normally based in local communities, rural or urban. They set out to provide health care, education, clean drinking water, irrigation, seeds and tools, training in carpentry, dressmaking and other skills. And they often combine many of these aims and more in an effort to meet the needs of a community in an integrated way.

There is a general expectation that local people will be involved in planning the projects and will contribute what they can — money, materials, labour — to the cost of carrying them out. The projects must meet their needs as they understand them, and clearly and primarily benefit them. Projects are usually funded for a limited number of years, after which it is hoped they will be self-supporting.

Typically projects are planned by a church-related development agency in the South, adopted and recommended by an ecumenical sponsor such as a national council of churches, then notified to the donor agencies in the North either directly or through the project lists of the World Council of Churches.

All-pervasive as they are, projects have been the target of considerable criticism. As early as 1971 some were saying that the project system was out-of-date and should come to an end. It still survives.

We shall leave one important criticism of projects — that they reflect the wrong kind of relationship between Northern agencies and Southern partners — for later discussion. What concerns us in this chapter is the way they have been constantly associated with "charity", "aid" and "service", all of which have been regarded as inadequate responses to poverty. According to the critics, the shortcomings of projects are not just potential but real. In short, they treat the symptoms but not the underlying causes. They may alleviate problems, but no matter how many projects are funded for however long, nothing fundamentally will change, and it is fundamental change that God and the poor require.

In many villages, projects funded by Christian Aid and other agencies have provided clean water, improving the health of the community and sparing women the long daily walk to fetch and carry water. But several years later the people remain desperately poor overall.

In the Palestinian refugee camps of Lebanon, women sew and embroider with the support of an organization funded by agencies like Christian Aid. They even earn a little money, but they remain materially poor, if not poor in spirit. They live in a strange land, where they have few rights or freedoms, and they cannot return to the country they call their own.

In the Great Lakes region of Central Africa, including Rwanda and Burundi, many communes receive support for farming and environmental projects designed not only to feed hungry people but to improve community relations or reconcile deeply divided factions. The deep ethnic divisions which drive them to war, fuelled by a desperate shortage of resources, remain.

Such stories are easily multiplied. The moral of them all is much the same. In terms of "charity", it has been summed up in the slogan "not charity but justice". The poor have a right to something more than condescending gifts provided from a surplus to which the wealthy often have little right. In terms of "aid", the concern is that it can be relatively short-term and superficial, offering little more than relief where long-term development is required. In terms of "service", the need is for "macro-diakonia" and not just "micro-diakonia": large horizons as well as small ones. We can have our sights set too narrowly and exclusively on the immediate need in front of us and fail to take a wider, more comprehensive view; in other words, a more strategic approach is required than "projects" and unrelated attempts to help a community here and a community there.

These and similar views find repeated expression in the ecumenical documents. One working group at the 1966 Geneva world conference on Church and Society, where the keynote was "justice not charity", insisted that "philanthropy at best can only be a balm for economic ills and at worst an opiate to postpone economic revolution". [1]

At a DICARWS consultation at Swanwick in 1966, Leslie Cooke warned that "it is possible for us to anaesthetize Christian people by engaging them in great aid programmes, thus dulling their sensitivities to the great uncomfortable and disturbing question of social and economic justice".

The same consultation believed that

> the service which the churches render to uprooted people will never pass the "ambulance" stage unless we study seriously the underlying causes of their movement. Such study will expose the injustices of the structures of our societies, and involve the churches in political decisions and actions. [2]

The fourth WCC assembly at Uppsala in 1968 challenged the churches to "move beyond the piecemeal and paternalistic programmes of charity which have sometimes characterized Christian mission, and... confront positively the systematic injustice of the world economy". [3] But for all its acute awareness of the radical changes needed to "make all things new", the assembly concluded that the project method adopted by DICARWS "is on the whole satisfactory"! [4]

The WCC's Commission on the Churches' Participation in Development (CCPD) intended from the start to go beyond "aid" projects, which it saw as "no more than patched up old structures", to a more comprehensive approach uniting the concepts of development and justice. Similarly, the WCC's 1973 world mission conference in Bangkok spoke of "the negative influence of the 'donor mentality' manifested in development aid ('help-syndrome'), thus perpetuating existing economic and political systems". [5]

In 1974 the consultation of CICARWS and CCPD in Montreux declared that

> the debate about development and the churches' involvement in development is still much too oriented towards project implementation and the transfer of aid. The churches — and not only those in the rich countries — must recognize the fact that the poor cannot be liberated through money. We consider that the present project system hinders the process of liberation. [6]

In a preparatory paper for the Nairobi assembly the next year, Richard Dickinson underscored that "more than charity and relief are required. Development and liberation require structural and systemic changes in political and economic institutions at both the national and international levels".[7]

A consultation organized by Church and Society and CCPD in Zurich in 1978 declared that "love" or "charity" was adequately understood only when linked to justice:

> The Latin equivalent of *agape*, *caritas*, is the source of the English word "charity", whose meaning has often been perverted in the churches. It has frequently been misinterpreted to mean optional, individual charity to those in need, without any reference to efforts to correct the structures which created that need. In our time, the concept has taken political economic shape as optional, voluntary aid from nation to nation. This can be no substitute for dealing with the international structures which give rise to the need.[8]

The link was made again by the CICARWS commission in the same year: "Our compassion for need leads to a passion for justice and structural change."[9]

Alexandros Papaderos in 1978 put forward the concepts of "micro-dimensional" and "macro-dimensional" diakonia, corresponding roughly to concrete responses to immediate need and structural change:

> Do we not sometimes have a feeling that the generally accepted patterns and methods of micro-dimensional therapeutic diakonia hardly represent more than just a means of maintaining the *status quo*...? Are not many charitable institutions (which do not always serve real needs!) little more than a sedative for the Christian conscience, a cover-up for social evils which are consciously or unconsciously ignored, an alibi for growing indifference?[10]

"Aid" was cast in the same mould as charity by CCPD's Advisory Group on Economic Matters when in 1979 it described aid as "at worst a palliative suppressing symptoms without treating structural causes".[11] Again in 1981 it reiterated that structural changes were more important than food aid: "Charity, when expressed in direct physical sharing or food, is obviously not enough, even though generous and blessed in itself. The challenge of hunger calls for much more."[12]

A resource-sharing consultation in Sofia in 1982 heard Istvan Nagy, a Lutheran from Hungary, stress in a lecture that

> service to the neighbour must not be limited to immediate help. It must also ask questions about structures of politics and society which are the root causes of any immediate need. A church which limits itself to dealing with the symptoms of need will, even politically, stabilize the forces of injustice. [13]

In 1989 the Africa diakonia consultation noted the increasing poverty of the continent and the way in which aid perpetuates dependency: "Diakonia as practised today often made the church an unconscious promoter of unjust systems... The old diaconal approach was too heavily orientated towards dealing with symptoms rather than root causes." [14]

Writing in an earlier review of the ecumenical response to poverty, Jean Fischer shows very clearly how the project system had been repeatedly questioned and criticized. He cites three papers: "Whither the project system?" (1973), "From projects to country programmes" (1975) and "Do we project ourselves in projects?" (1977), as well as a memorandum expressing his own unease as early as 1971, when he wrote to the then-director of CICARWS:

> The project system has now been operating for nearly twenty years... Many projects have been formulated, financed and implemented... but in a dispersed order..., independently from one to another, often for prestige reasons or for denominational interests. Little overall planning has been done and one rightly ought to ask whether such projects have had a sizeable impact on national situations... The types of projects proposed by the churches have not always been responses to critical problems of the national communities... Few projects have aimed at treating the root causes of underdevelopment such as agrarian reform, workers' unions, farmers' unions and cooperatives, housing, unemployment and other "justice" concerns. [15]

In the hope of radical change, Fischer proposed a moratorium on projects for two years.

The persistence of "charity"

Looking back, the main criticisms of "charity" are clear enough. They have been rehearsed repeatedly over the last 50 years. They have to do chiefly with the relationships between givers and receivers (to which we shall return), a lack of strategy and a neglect of underlying causes. Why then has this way of responding persisted and remained so attractive?

Part of the answer lies in the manageable scale of projects. They are limited to particular communities or issues. They run for a limited number of years. They have boundaries: a beginning and an end. They can be comprehended. In contrast, once the interrelatedness of poverty issues is opened up and questions are asked about its causes, there seems to be no end in sight. In that context, the problem of poverty is so overwhelming that the feeling among those whose hearts are moved shifts from being able to do "at least something", even if "it's only a little", to being powerless and being able to do nothing at all of any consequence. [16]

Resistance to a more fundamental attack on poverty also arises from the perception that the changes required will involve *us*. Charitable support for limited projects can be funded without too much pain out of the surplus of better-off individuals and nations. Gustavo Gutiérrez suggested at the SODEPAX conference in Cartigny in 1969 that "this aid might also be able to offer, at a cheap price, a good conscience to Christians, citizens of countries that control the world economy". [17] Our wealth is left basically untouched. A fairer distribution of resources in the name of justice could be a much more costly venture. Even if it may not be true that the poor can benefit only at the expense of the rich (often referred to as a "zero-sum game"), many believe that this is the case and thus do not alter their cautious, conservative behaviour.

The change that could come with a more radical response to poverty could also threaten our whole way of working as agencies within the ecumenical family. It could challenge what Jean Fischer described as "a whole network of well-oiled and well-tried operations". [18] It could require new ways of relating and taking decisions which might rob us of the independence and control we have long enjoyed. Vested interests in our institutions are at stake.

Politics

Feeling overwhelmed and feeling threatened are also huge sources of energy which fuel the ongoing debates about Christianity and politics and charity and politics. Theology can easily be used to dress up actions, or the failure to act, after the event and turn understandable fears into high-principled positions. And most people are nervous of politics. It is seen as a complex and dubious business. Charity is safer, less disruptive and less controversial. However, not all the arguments in favour of churches and charitable agencies keeping out of politics are bogus. To understand why we often mount them with enthusiasm is not to say they have no validity.

The debate is certainly long-running. To take an example, in the 1980s it surfaced memorably for Christian Aid in the United Kingdom over apartheid and the often bitterly argued view that sanctions against South Africa were the least damaging and most promising "peaceful" means of putting an end to it and to the humiliation and abject poverty it had brought to the vast majority of South Africa's people. It was an argument which Christian Aid supported as a member of a wide coalition of charities, churches, trade unions, student and other organizations.

When supporters of Christian Aid and others insisted that we should "keep politics out of it", some of their arguments were not of much substance. They were the children of fear and vested interest. Or they were ways not of objecting to politics as such but to what was judged to be the wrong politics. What was to be kept out was the political point of view with which the objectors happened to disagree.

Some of the arguments were familiar enough. One centred on the duty of the church and its adherents, including its agencies, to obey the powers that be, ordained as they are by God (Romans 13). In other words, "don't criticize or undermine the policies of the government with your protests and campaigns." The policy of the British government was to minimize international sanctions against South Africa, and its own observance of those that did exist was reluctant to the point that its compliance was virtually non-existent. A second had to do with claims about the "proper" sphere of the church's concern, namely with the spiritual rather than the material, the private rather than the public, the inner soul of the person rather than outward political and economic structures.

Where the argument became more interesting was when it dealt with the competence of a church or a charity. The point made was that the church may be perfectly competent to derive certain principles from its faith, such as insisting that all human beings are equally important to God and are to be treated as such, even if all are not equally gifted. The church may be competent to test certain policies and practices against these principles, including apartheid, and find them severely wanting on that basis alone. But the church has no way of deriving from these general principles detailed political policies and vesting them with its authority. Even if its principles are beyond question there are too many other considerations affecting detailed policies which are not. They range from the accompanying circumstances which suggest what is and is not appropriate, to technical knowledge and experience of what will or will not work. People will disagree about these even if they agree about the underlying principles. There is thus, according to the argument, no such thing as a "Christian" policy.

This conclusion is and is not true. There is probably no single policy which is irrefutably the only possible one which a church and its adherents can uphold with integrity. There is probably no detailed policy to which all will or must agree as the obvious conclusion to be drawn from their faith. Nevertheless, there may sometimes be a consensus shared by a large number of Christians; and even if there is not, it may be the duty of Christians to work out detailed policies provided they do not claim too much for them or seal them off from criticism and debate. Otherwise they will take no concrete actions in the world at all.

Charities and politics

The argument that charities (as distinct from churches) should keep out of politics because they may not be competent was mounted by the Charity Commission, the legal watchdog on charities in England and Wales. In the end it required charities like Christian Aid to withdraw from membership of the coalition which was actively supporting sanctions against South Africa.

As a matter of fact, charities in England and Wales, while they may not have political objectives, may get involved in political *activities* — that is, activities which aim to uphold or change the laws of the country or the policies of its government — provided that those laws or policies are directly relevant to the charity's "objects" or reasons for existing, such as the relief of poverty. These objects have to be charitable.

Even so, charities may get involved only on certain conditions. Their political activities must not get out of proportion; in other words, Christian Aid should not spend more time and money on political campaigning than it does on the direct relief of poverty. Moreover, they must put the case for a particular policy in a balanced way (an especially difficult requirement for those who believe they should have an unbalanced "bias" towards the poor!). Yet another condition is that they seek allies not by emotional crusades but by reasoned explanation.

The interesting question of competence re-emerges when it comes to the requirement that the policies being pursued must be policies that will benefit the charity's beneficiaries, in this case the poor of the Third World. Thus, for example, to campaign for the forgiveness of Third World debt is open to question because, even if debt obligations are cancelled, the gains for Third World governments may not be passed on to the poorest but only into the coffers of the elite; and the credibility of a country in terms of its economic obligations may be so undermined by debt forgiveness that would-be investors are frightened off and it remains as unproductive and unable to help its people as before.

But it was not just debt forgiveness or some such particular policy that was questioned. It was any political policy whatever, since all of them were judged to be unpredictable and uncertain in their outcome. Since a charity is not competent to judge that its political activities will be of any use to those it claims to serve, it should keep out of them altogether. In the case of South Africa, many, including politicians, felt competent enough to claim the opposite. They argued that sanctions were wrong because sanctions would actually harm the poor by depressing the South African economy even further and throwing even more people out of work.

Later the guidelines of the Charity Commission were revised to talk about the need for "reasonable expectations" that a political policy would help to fulfil the aims of the charity. [19] But the nub of the argument about whether or not the charity should get involved in political activity remains the question of competence to judge what will be of benefit.

Walking on two legs

There is one further reason why the project system and all it
stands for in terms of charity, "micro-diakonia" and aid has survived
despite persistent criticism; and that is because it has some validity.
Taken by itself it will not do. But as a partner in what might be
called a two-legged approach, it has a role to play. Even if it fails to
change the structures, it does meet immediate human needs. It
supports human struggles for survival which, however localized,
cannot wait for the grand structural solutions which love is bound to
pursue and which when found will not solve everything. The project
system has its achievements. It has improved people's quality of life.
It may even tip the scales a little in favour of justice in wholly
oppressive situations. And is there any reason why "projects",
somewhat discrete in themselves, cannot be shaped in such as way as
to contribute to a wider strategy for change? For all their constant
questioning, the ecumenical documents concede some of these
points.

As early as 1937, for example, the Oxford conference on Life and
Work included this interesting remark in its report:

> There is no legal, political or economic system so bad or so good as to
> absolve individuals from the responsibility to transcend its requirements
> by acts of Christian charity... Individual acts of charity within a given
> system of government or economics may mitigate its injustices and
> increase its justice. But they do not absolve the Christian from seeking the
> best possible institutional arrangement and social structure for the order-
> ing of human life. [20]

A 1965 DICARWS consultation in preparation for the Geneva
Church and Society conference the next year concluded that

> the challenge of the contemporary revolution to the churches' "diakonia"
> today is to develop new policies, new concepts, new forms of action
> which will, on the one hand, continue to meet individual, family and
> wider social needs, and, on the other, to promote social justice on a
> community or national or ecumenical world basis rather than on a strictly
> personal one. [21]

While fully aware of the need for structural change, Leslie Cooke
reminded the DICARWS consultation in Swanwick, England, in 1966
of some words of Visser 't Hooft:

There is little consolation for the hungry, homeless, poverty-stricken, disease-ridden man suffering now in the knowledge that his children or grandchildren may have a better life. We ought not to hesitate to give this answer to those who criticize the compassionate or charitable aspects of this task. [22]

The WCC assembly at Uppsala in 1968 advocated that at least one percent of the Gross National Product (GNP) of developed nations be "made available as aid to the developing". To that extent it upheld the role of charity but only within a framework of "equitable patterns of trade and investment". [23]

In 1973 a memorandum of the Evangelical Church in Germany saw compassion and the work for justice as belonging together: "compassion and justice, service to individuals and society as a whole, the elimination of the causes of injustice as well as the care for the victims of such injustice are all alike signs of the good news of the coming of God's kingdom". [24]

In 1986 a joint working group on Koinonia-Diakonia saw the importance of an immediate short-term curative diakonia as well as a long-term, preventive diakonia. A booklet published by ICCO in the Netherlands somewhat turned the tables on those who argued only for fundamental change in the name of justice:

> Strife against injustice and for structural change is not enough. It is of fundamental importance for our hungering, thirsting, naked and homeless fellow-man that we are compassionate towards him in his situation from which there often appears to be no escape. [25]

The WCC consultations at Larnaca and El Escorial in 1986 and 1987, and its world convocation on Justice, Peace and the Integrity of Creation in Seoul in 1990 gave support to a "two-legged approach". Following Larnaca CICARWS acknowledged in a report to the WCC executive committee that "charity is necessary in certain circumstances" but that its work must be "a challenge to unjust structures". Seoul, while recognizing "that the needs of 'the least' can only be met by fundamentally transforming the world economy through structural change", nevertheless supported "the need for diaconal services and urgent response to emergencies". [26]

Perhaps this "two-legged" image can help to understand the relation within the WCC between CCPD and CICARWS (Unit III and

Unit IV since 1993). It has not always been an easy one. The very existence of CCPD could be understood as embodying all the criticisms and reservations about the kind of Christian service to the needy associated with CICARWS. The consultation in Montreux in 1970 out of which CCPD arose had engaged in a critique of the ecumenical response to poverty and decided that a more comprehensive approach was required; and the WCC executive committee approved the establishment of the new Commission on the Churches' Participation in Development the following month.

As time went on, CCPD talked a great deal about solidarity and people's movements, sounding even further away than ever from the language of charitable projects. It could be seen as more radical than CICARWS, more interested in issues, more eager to debate theories of development and intellectually more substantial in its reports. For example, its study process on "The Church and the Poor" and the volumes which came out of it — *To Set at Liberty the Oppressed* (1975), *Good News to the Poor*, *Separation Without Hope* and *Towards a Church of the Poor* — are nowhere paralleled in the work of CICARWS (understandably so, since such tasks were deliberately given to CCPD). [27] The consultation in Larnaca in 1986 pressed for a review of the relationship between the two.

Still, the divide between the two should not be exaggerated. CICARWS continually made statements about justice and the need for structural change. The two cooperated from the start. The limitations to what CICARWS could do were recognized and understood. The consultation on "The Struggle of the Poor for Social Justice and Liberation" in Montreux in 1974 was called jointly by CICARWS and CCPD and, among other things, called for spending half of the programme budgets of each on people's movements for changing structures in the rich societies. In 1984 they jointly established the round table structure, though the move was seen as a clear indication of the impact of "CCPD thinking" on the structures of inter-church aid.

For a time both CICARWS and CCPD were sub-units within Unit II of the WCC. It looked like a sensible division of labour, involving CCIA (Commission of the Churches on International Affairs) and URM (Urban and Rural Mission), as well as CCPD and CICARWS, within an holistic understanding of a shared task. For the agencies which related more to CICARWS than CCPD, it was not so straight-forward. Some could look realistically to other organizations to work for underlying change and so complement their own contribution; others could not and were therefore more directly challenged to take on the dual role themselves. Since 1993, CCPD has been identified with Unit III (Justice, Peace and Creation) and CICARWS with Unit IV (Sharing and Service). The link has to some extent been broken but relations have been improved.

If there are good reasons why Unit IV should now give up most of its work on projects, the argument that this form of support for the poorest of the poor has no place whatever in the response to poverty is not one of them.

The real division of opinion or difference in emphasis has less to do with CCPD and CICARWS than with the views of the North and the South. The North with its agencies has been the more articulate of the two in its support for maintaining compassionate service and for co-opting it into the cause for justice. The more radical and question-ing voices have most often been those of the developing countries. And if we are to walk on two legs we had better recognize — at the risk of overworking the metaphor — that we do not walk all that steadily. One leg is far weaker than the other. We limp!

Setting about change

But how do we set about the more fundamental structural changes that are required in the name of justice, macro-diakonia and long-term development? The answers thrown up by the ecu-menical family over the last 50 years can probably be pared down to two: universalizing the "success" of Western technology and capitalism on the one hand, or being in solidarity with the poor on the other — an industrial revolution or a social or political revolution. The long-running confrontation between the two was reflected in the very title as well as the proceedings of the WCC's world conference on Church and Society in Geneva in 1966: "Christians in the Technical and Social Revolutions of Our Time". It is a confrontation which for the time being at least appears to have been won by the West.

It may be helpful to deal with the question of change not under two headings but five: (1) the attempt to be more strategic; (2) sharing the achievements of capitalism; (3) creating new visions of society; (4) reforming the system; and (5) solidarity with the poor.

1. The attempt to be more strategic

Projects are said to fail to deal with the underlying causes of poverty because they are "un-strategic" in two senses. First, they are too parochial, treating the ills of a community as if the sources of its troubles were largely within the community itself when in fact they are largely due to outside forces which will prove stronger and more enduring than any local achievement. Local production, for example, is of limited value without stable, accessible and profitable markets.

Second, projects are insufficiently related to each other, so that they fail to make a significant difference overall. More strategic are "multipliers", where lessons learned in one place are readily transferred to another. So is "concentration", where attention is focused on one particular sector, such as the provision of clean water, or one issue, such as drought, which is seen as the key to many other improvements over a wider area. Instead of dissipating energy and limited resources on many things there is a concerted effort to get one very important thing right at a time. Such a strategy was proposed by SEARCH in India in 1992.

Round tables, regionalization, national forums and the country policy papers which are their counterparts within the funding agencies can be seen as attempts to put projects within the context of wider, more strategic plans.

Round table structures were originally called for at a WCC consultation at Crêt-Bérard, Switzerland, in 1984 as a better way of sharing power and decision-making over the use of resources. Regional groups, which go back as far as 1972, assumed greater importance as the concept of resource-sharing was elaborated, particularly after the Larnaca conference in 1986 with its emphasis on regionalization, and the El Escorial conference in 1987. They were to serve a purpose similar to that of the round tables. Round tables brought North and South, agencies, mission boards and what were often national councils of churches face-to-face to discuss a wide-ranging programme and decide how it should be funded. The relationship was to be one of mutual respect and shared responsibilities. The result could be agreements to fund all or parts of a programme, and "priority projects" which were subsequently listed and published by CICARWS and in theory picked up by others not present at the table and funded without further ado. Priority projects were said to be of first importance for the work in hand; it did not however always mean they were the most strategic.

Round table and regional group meetings were often criticized for being narrowly preoccupied with money, and money for one particular organization which should have seen its role as representing many and varied churches and interests within a national ecumenical family rather than promoting its own interests. A review of round tables was instituted by Unit IV in 1994. Recent years have seen attempts to shift the focus of discussion away from money to broader considerations. What are the problems facing the country? What are their internal and external causes? How should they be tackled and in what order? What contribution could each of the interested parties make to the whole plan, and what help from others would they need? In other words, funding decisions should be made in the light of careful analysis and an agreed plan.

A concern for strategic planning was voiced again, especially by representatives of the South, when four Northern agencies related to the WCC (Christian Aid, ICCO — Interchurch Organization for Development Cooperation, Netherlands, Bread for the World and EZE — Protestant Association for Cooperation in Development) tried in 1993 to evaluate their work and see ways forward in a programme of study called "Discerning the Way Together" (see Chapter 6 below). This time the planning was to be done not by round tables but by national forums, which were to be more inclusive than round tables, drawing in all the non-governmental organizations committed to overcoming poverty, and not just the churches.

Regional group meetings were to develop a sense of priorities on an even bigger scale and be even further removed from immediate funding issues. They were charged with issuing guidelines which all bilateral funding of programmes and projects was then committed to respect. The chief difficulty has been developing any guidelines which are sufficiently concrete and relevant to have enough bite to make a difference. The groups have lacked the information and data required to make a meaningful and not just an anecdotal analysis.

Within the agencies a shift towards becoming more strategic can be discerned in the development of country policy papers and programmes. These papers are drawn up in consultation with partners. Often the same partners are drawn into similar planning exercises by several agencies — the sort of wasteful duplication which national forums, for all their difficulties, might avoid. A typical policy paper offers some political, social and economic analysis; a strategic plan indicating where special attention should be given to certain parts of the country, certain groups and certain issues (for example, sustainable agriculture or gender); and a survey of the players in the field and their present and potential contributions. Once the policy is agreed, grants to particular partners and projects are considered in the light of it.

One other device which can be used to push isolated projects into a more strategic framework is the use of criteria or development project guidelines ("DPGs" as they were called by some agencies). These are not sufficient without overall strategic plans, but they can help. If a project, whether it has to do with health or education or agriculture or whatever, is readily multiplied, if it tackles gender issues, if it trains those involved to be better managers of people and resources, if it fosters networks and inter-connections whereby people can share their knowledge and organize and lend their strengths to one another, it will probably be more "strategic" than a project which does not.

2. *Sharing the achievements of capitalism*

Beyond national and regional plans there has long been an international strategy to deal with the underlying causes of poverty, namely to multiply or reproduce the economic achievements of the Western world. It is often referred to as modernization. Its good intentions were embodied in the Bretton Woods institutions — World Bank, International Monetary Fund, General Agreement on Tariffs and Trade (GATT), now the World Trade Organization — over 50 years ago. The strategy is as firmly in place as ever it was. While dangers were recognized from the beginning,[28] a great deal of faith was put in the spread of technology, industry and economic growth rather than "charity" as the key to "justice" and an end to the worst of poverty.

The second WCC assembly at Evanston in 1954 was full of praise for economic and technical aid, describing "the response of more developed countries through expanded international programmes of technical assistance" as "one of the brightest pages of recent history" — even if, it concluded, "the effort thus far has been small in comparison with the needs of the less developed countries and the resources of those more developed". [29]

Economic and technical aid was linked to other issues such as trade by a consultation on "The Specific European Responsibilities in Relation to Africa and Asia" in Odense, Denmark in 1958, but it was nevertheless seen as the most important European responsibility.

The WCC conference on "Christian Action in Rapid Social Change: Dilemmas and Opportunities" at Thessalonica, Greece, in 1959 drew together the four-year Church and Society study programme on "Our Common Christian Responsibility Towards Areas of Rapid Social Change". It had much to say about Christian responsibility for economic development. Referring to Odense, it recognized that "these responsibilities include not only technical aid and financial help (perhaps as a given proportion of national income), but also a recognition and correction of the ill effects on the poorer countries of Western policies" — for example in the areas of immigration, tariffs and subsidies, commodity prices, defence — "and the whole trend of industrial development towards more or less self-sufficiency". It agreed with Odense that the contribution of the rich countries to economic development in Africa, Asia and Latin America was totally inadequate; and it agreed that modern technology makes the eradication of poverty possible, if only it is shared. [30]

A similar faith shines through several reports of the WCC assembly in New Delhi in 1961, though it warned against undue emphasis on material progress.

Technological development promises liberation from hunger, disease and misery...

In the specific field of economic development, we welcome the vigorous effort to increase production and raise living standards... It is a matter of gratification that many of the more advanced nations have sought to aid the progress of the economically less developed countries...

There is a great opportunity for constructive action in the struggle for world development. To share the benefits of civilization with the whole of humanity is a noble and obtainable objective... [calling for] a far

greater commitment of scientific, educational and material resources than
hitherto... But above all the churches must not cease to champion the
cause of making the riches of the developed countries available to those
poor in resources. [31]

At the 1966 Church and Society conference in Geneva opinion
was divided. There was another point of view, to which we must
come. Even the traditional view raised plenty of ethical questions, but
the need to share the economic and technical achievements of the
West with the developing world was nevertheless upheld by the
conference section which discussed "Economic Development in a
World Perspective":

> The churches should welcome economic growth because it helps to free
> men from unnecessary want and economic insecurity. Economic growth
> in the relatively few richer nations of the world makes it incumbent on
> them to assist in the enormous task of helping the developing countries to
> move along the road to self-sustained development. This is the biggest
> issue in the world today, and it will be with us for generations to come. [32]

At a conference in Beirut in 1968, organized jointly by the
Pontifical Commission on Justice and Peace and the WCC, development was still seen very much in economic terms and as a technical
problem of growth, but it was to be resolved mainly by experts within
the developing countries:

> The developing countries must achieve a much more rapid rate of
> growth...; the basic responsibility for development will continue to lie
> with the developing countries themselves...; their own leaders will have
> to mobilize and inspire their people and work against the traditions,
> structures and political forces standing in the way of economic and social
> progress.

If the onus was placed on unexpected shoulders, it remained the
responsibility of the richer countries to promote "just political and
economic structures, and just sharing of our talents, our resources and
our riches". [33]

World poverty was one of the dominant themes of the fourth WCC
assembly at Uppsala in 1968. Tensions similar to those which
emerged at Geneva were again apparent. Revolutionary and economic
themes were combined in calls for more "equitable patterns of trade
and investment". Some, like André Philip, spoke mainly of develop-

ment as technical improvement and rather paternalistically of the Third World needing "our support and help". Others, like Samuel Parmar, looked for political self-reliance and social justice and "radical alterations in the values and structures of society".

The report of the assembly section on "World Economic and Social Development" brought the two views together to some extent with a call "to participate in the struggle of millions of people for greater social justice and for world development" that is, economic development. "Christians should promote social policies in which the technological revolution will redress the balance between the poor and the rich rather than merely make the rich richer". [34] Uppsala, however, remained of two minds.

Since the late 1960s there has probably been more criticism than praise within ecumenical circles for economic and technical development and for reproducing the Western economic system with its economic successes in the South. Economic "globalization" has become suspect. The Western system, it is claimed, has generally disappointed the hopes of the poor. By drawing them into the system it has made them poorer. [35] It perpetuates the South's dependence and the North's dominance. "Affluence is not liberation" even where it is achieved. [36] CCPD soon included fewer technical experts among the members of its commission and turned to different strategies. [37]

Beyond WCC circles faith in economic growth and the ability of the Western economic system to succeed on a universal scale has, if anything, grown. Some would say it has "triumphed". There are long and deep arguments about its sustainability and its ability to distribute the wealth it creates but, despite the doubts, the widespread effort to draw the developing countries into a single free-market capitalist economy with the industrially and technologically advanced is generally seen as the key to worldwide growth and prosperity.

3. Creating new visions of society

Insofar as the change required to tackle poverty was not seen simply as the reproduction of Western technology, industrialization and economic growth ("modernization") in the South, whatever the benefits, but as the creation of a new social and economic order, what was this new social order to be like? Several suggestions can be found in the ecumenical documents, most notably: the Responsible Society, a New International Economic Order, a Just and Sustainable Society, a Just, Participatory and Sustainable Society and — if it is a model — Justice, Peace and Integrity of Creation. The Responsible Society was described at the WCC assembly at Evanston in 1954 as being

> not an alternative social or political system, but a criterion by which we judge all existing social orders and at the same time a standard to guide us in the specific choices we have to make.[38]

It was defined earlier at Amsterdam in 1948 as a society in which

> freedom is the freedom of men who acknowledge responsibility to justice and public order, and in which those who hold public authority or economic power are responsible for its exercise to God and the people whose welfare is affected by it.[39]

The Responsible Society had its merits but was criticized for sounding too much like Western democracies, for allowing too much to the status quo in preference to revolutionary change and for stressing political but not economic justice. At Evanston the pursuit of it was contrasted to "irresponsible" attempts to do quickly what the West had taken centuries to achieve. Communist revolutions were very much in mind![40] African, Asian and Latin American participants in the Geneva conference of 1966 criticized the Responsible Society as a concept intended to provide theological sanction for the Western concept of democracy. Trying to meet such criticisms, the Uppsala assembly in 1968 spoke of working for "a worldwide responsible society".[41]

By the time of the Nairobi assembly in 1975, the term Responsible Society had given way to Just, Participatory and Sustainable Society. In the previous year, President Julius Nyerere of Tanzania had introduced the concept of "sustainability" as a challenge to accelerating economic growth. A Church and Society conference in Bucharest in 1974 recommended that the WCC sponsor a study of a just and sustainable society.[42] Charles Birch said at Nairobi that it "demands a fundamental change of heart and mind about humankind's relation to nature" — a hint of the later theme of the "integrity of creation".[43] Once again Nairobi did not present a pattern or blueprint but was for the most part a commentary on how a more just society is brought about, namely by the empowerment of the people. It did not describe the end so much as the means, a theme to which we shall return in the section on solidarity with the poor below (pp.71-73).

The need for a blueprint or "a new paradigm that would correspond to the operational requirements of a just, participatory and sustainable society and inspire new understanding of the dimensions of poverty in the world and the demands of the gospel" was referred to in a consultation organized by Church and Society and CCPD in Zurich in 1978, but it was not spelled out. [44] It was further debated in 1979 by CCPD, by the WCC central committee (which was divided over a report it received on the subject) and at the Church and Society conference at the Massachusetts Institute of Technology (MIT) in Cambridge, USA.

"The New International Economic Order" was the title of a document prepared by CCPD for the WCC central committee meeting in Geneva in 1977. It was a phrase which had currency far beyond the churches. It was referred to at Nairobi [45] and of course in the later Brandt Report, *North-South: A Programme for Survival.* The search for it, which "should be seen as part of the calling of the churches" seems to be identical with the "search for a just, participatory and sustainable society". [46] The world mission conference in Melbourne in 1980 also used the phrase, though in a very general way:

> The churches have to exercise the prophetic gift of assessing the effectiveness of the various socio-economic systems in the world and speak in favour of exploratory models of a new international economic order in the light of the thrust of the gospel. [47]

For the WCC's Vancouver assembly in 1983, the phrase once again echoed the earlier concern with participation: "We urgently need a new international economic order in which power is shared, not grasped. We are committed to work for it." [48] The same goes for the Larnaca consultation in 1986:

> Economic and social structures which perpetuate inequality and poverty must be replaced by a new international economic order and political structure which ensures the full participation of all people in the decisions which affect their lives. [49]

"Justice, Peace and Integrity of Creation" has been much discussed in WCC circles since the Vancouver assembly, though, on the evidence of the documents, less so among those in the forefront of the ecumenical response to poverty. El Escorial affirmed it as the value system which was to inspire its guidelines for sharing, and it gave its name to a world convocation in Seoul in 1990. The Canberra assembly in 1991 gathered some of the fruits of what had been called "a conciliar process" and discussed how "social justice and ecologically responsible human behaviour" might be achieved, not least by reforming the international economic order and basing it on co-operation rather than competition. [50]

To the concern for sustainable growth and use of resources has been added a respect for nature. Sometimes nature seems to be conceived of as a given, satisfactory and integrated whole — a unity of which human beings are a part — which is not to be tampered with. Probably it is more accurately to be regarded as a complex and inter-related phenomenon which involves human beings and is to be treated with great care and understanding, sacred but not sacrosanct. Reluctance in certain ecumenical quarters to discuss the "integrity of creation" may reflect the initial ambivalence of the "poverty lobby" towards the environmental debate, which they saw as too easily becoming a distraction afforded by the better-off rather than a dimension of their own concerns. The inter-connections between poverty and environmental degradation are now more readily appreciated.

In conclusion, talk of new visions of society in the ecumenical documents has underlined the need for alternatives and drawn out some of the general criteria — responsible, participatory, sustainable, etc. — by which they are to be judged; but for all the many calls to modify and reform the old structures, there have been far fewer ideas about what any new structures might look like if they could be achieved. [51]

4. Reforming the system

Reform rather than revolution, adjusting the existing order rather than replacing it with another one, is a fourth way in which the ecumenical family has "become political" in seeking to deal with the underlying or structural causes of poverty. The chief targets have been patterns of trade and the international financial system, including the problem of debt.

At the DICARWS world consultation in Swanwick in 1966, Samuel Parmar had difficulty in distinguishing between such reforms and revolutions: "To be involved in national development programmes is to be involved in revolution," he argued, that is, in radical, structural change:

> It is not enough to plead for increased aid. It is even more important to work for conditions for greater trade with greater fairness. If the church is engaged in national development it cannot remain silent about some of the iniquitous patterns of trade and aid... Those who help hungry children in Asia or Africa must not hold back from purchasing goods from these areas — even if it means affecting their [own] structures of production and employment. [52]

In 1971 CCPD, recognizing the "systemic character" of underdevelopment, set aside 25 percent of its budget for development education so that the better-off could better understand the reforms they needed to bring about.

In November 1984, CCPD's Advisory Group on Economic Matters discussed "The International Financial System". While recognizing that the success of aid programmes in many countries gave grounds for confidence, it also put forward proposals for reform based on the values of "fulfilment of basic physical and spiritual needs; justice; self-reliance; sustainability; globability; equity for the most vulnerable; and furtherance of peace." It added that

> the basic action responsibility of Christians, Christian organizations and churches must lie in identifying principles relevant to and means for transforming or reforming the international financial system. Churches are not of the international financial system's world, but they must recognize that they are in it and have a duty to change it. [53]

El Escorial (October 1987) was perhaps calling for more than reform when it spoke of "a new economic and political order" and the need to "resist international mechanisms (such as the International Monetary Fund and the World Bank) which deprive the people of the South of their resources" and for "radical change in global and local structures". It was not enough, it declared, to improve the aid system, since "on the whole, the international aid system is not able to change the trend of increasing poverty and marginalization". [54]

The WCC's 1989 world conference on mission and evangelism spoke of the suffering of countries because of the debt crisis, as did the world convocation on Justice, Peace and the Integrity of Creation in

Seoul in 1990, which pledged itself to work towards "the establishment of a just structure of the international financial system" where "people come first" and to support "activities which aim at exposing the causes and effects of the international debt crisis". [55]

The WCC assembly in Canberra in 1991 called for changes which "will come only by active opposition and informed and responsible social pressure":

> Particularly the churches in industrialized countries must put great pressure on their governments to establish just patterns of trade and to share their resources with the poorer nations. Initiatives should be taken to overcome the international debt crisis. Control of the immense power of the global corporations still presents the largest challenge at international levels of decision-making. [56]

The Asia Regional Group meeting in Colombo in 1994 called once again for the cancellation of debt, fair prices in trade and economic systems "re-designed to distribute wealth fairly, not just to create it at any price".

These continuous calls for reform have been echoed by agencies, including Christian Aid. Like others, it has long emphasized the importance of development education so that the causes of poverty are understood. It has campaigned in alliances and networks with other organizations, on debt, trade and the policies of the World Bank and the IMF. In the early 1990s it encouraged its supporters, as customers of British "High Street" banks, to challenge them to ease the burden of debt repayment on Third World countries. It supported the British government's proposals to the Group of Seven industrialized countries (G7) in the form of the "Trinidad Terms" for dealing with the debts of some of the poorest and middle-income countries. It helped to create consumer demand for fairly-traded goods in supermarkets. It challenged the policy of what was then the European Community of dumping subsidized beef and other products on Third World markets, thereby undermining local trade. It engaged in the debate on the Uruguay round of negotiations of the GATT (General Agreement on Tariffs and Trade). It alerted British taxpayers to the fact that their money supports the World Bank and the IMF, whose policies, particularly in the area of structural adjustment, harm rather than help many of the world's poor. All of this, it is fair to say, amounts to attempts to reform a system — namely the system of free-market capitalism — which otherwise remains in place and which many assume has proved its worth and is here to stay especially, in their judgment, since the "Asian Tigers" and "NICs" (or Newly Industrialized Countries) seem to be proving that it can work even in previously underdeveloped countries.

5. *Solidarity with the poor*

"Solidarity with the poor" is often heard as revolutionary language — revolutionary as to the extent of change, the manner in which it is brought about or both.

If we are talking about the extent of change, there have been many voices urging the ecumenical family to go beyond reform to revolution. Some of them were clearly heard at the Geneva conference in 1966. Development as it was being understood was not enough. More radical changes were required.

Samuel Parmar, speaking at Uppsala in 1968, would accept "development" only if defined in these radical and revolutionary terms: "It is revolution... because it... breaks up old institutions to create new, brings about radical alterations in the values and structures of society". [57] He returned to this theme in Montreux in 1970:

Development cannot take place without radical changes in economic and social relationships, and diffusion of political power. Such changes are accompanied by instability, disorder, upheaval. We completely misunderstand the process of development if we equate it with static stability. Thus understood, development is revolution. [58]

At the meeting organized by SODEPAX in 1969, Gustavo Gutiérrez questioned the concept of "development" — in favour of the concept of "liberation" — warning that

economic aid, if it is not well oriented, could easily be unproductive in respect of the witness to poverty... It may also lead... to a reformist position producing superficial social changes which in the long run will only help to prolong the situation of misery and of injustice in which the marginalized people live. [59]

The WCC central committee meeting in Berlin in 1974 approved the CCIA report "Economic Threats to Peace", which also looked for more radical and revolutionary change: "The transformation demanded goes beyond modification of existing international economic structures, which perpetuate under-development and intensify the threat to peace, to the establishment of the new, just alternative system."[60]

If we are talking about revolution not in terms of the extent of change but in terms of how change is brought about, the ecumenical family has been far more reticent. Geneva 1966 acknowledged that revolution "has a solid foundation in Christian tradition and should have its rightful place in the life of the church and in the ongoing discussion of social responsibility". But this was not how many (who were doubtless less frustrated) saw it:

> As Christians, we are committed to working for the transformation of society. In the past, we have usually done this through quiet efforts at social renewal, working in and through the established institutions according to their rules.[61]

The ambiguities of the outcome, as of remaining within the rules, were acknowledged. Evanston counselled against revolution. Uppsala undeniably felt the weight of its challenge. The issue of armed struggle, of violence and non-violence, added yet another disturbing dimension to the debate.

However, one answer to the question about how radical or revolutionary change is brought about, reorganizing rather than merely adjusting society, seemed clear. It is not apparently through those who already have power and influence but through the growing contribution of those who do not. "Real development can no longer be conceived apart from a people's movement for liberation and social justice... People's participation... must therefore be basic to the work of the churches in fostering social change."[62]

The WCC Nairobi assembly in 1975 saw development as "joining hands with all who are engaged in the task of organizing the poor in their fight against poverty and injustice";[63] and CCPD subsequently urged the churches "to manifest in their theological outlook, styles of life and organizational structures their solidarity with the struggle of the poor and the oppressed" (which is not necessarily the same as the participation of the poor themselves!).[64] The point was made more clearly in *Towards a Church of the Poor*, published in 1979, which stressed that Christians do not work *for* the poor but *with* the poor. Development cannot be done for them. It can only be achieved by them when they become full participants in the processes which lead to justice and liberation.[65]

The Church and Society conference at MIT in 1979 saw the

> need to understand what is happening in the world so that people may find ways of transforming and humanizing the structures (the principalities and powers). Such transformation is not possible without participation at the appropriate level from local communities all the way through to the whole world.[66]

Larnaca 1986 recognized "that justice will not be given by the powerful until and unless the powerless stand together", that is unless there is solidarity of the poor as well as with the poor.[67] The Africa Diakonia consultation of April 1989 also underlined that solidarity with the poor had to mean the participation of the poor, "otherwise it turns into a one-way charity".[68]

Talk about more radical changes brought about by "solidarity" and participation clearly raised sharp issues of power; and where talk about "politics" or structural change and "power" come together, as they must — and as they did, for example, in the WCC's Programme to Combat Racism, set up in 1969 — Christians often become even more ill at ease and convinced that their Christianity is more at home in the less controversial and safer world of charity. Their cry is the same as that of yet another would-be donor to Christian Aid on yet another doorstep in Christian Aid Week: "Keep politics out of it". Yet it is to issues of power that we must now turn. Meanwhile, our review of the ecumenical family's constant and in many respects welcome cry for structural and political change to eradicate poverty has left behind a measure of disappointment at the lack of thoroughly worked out, concrete proposals as to what viable alternative economic orders, whether radically new or reformed, might actually look like.

NOTES

[1] *Christians in the Technical and Social Revolutions of Our Time*, Geneva, WCC, 1967, p.210.
[2] *Digest of the 1966 World Consultation on Inter-Church Aid*, Geneva, WCC, 1966, pp.39, 113.
[3] N. Goodall, ed., *Uppsala 68 Speaks*, Geneva, WCC, 1968, p.68.

4 N. Goodall, ed., *Uppsala Report*, Geneva, WCC, 1968, p.256.

5 Minutes of the Bangkok assembly 1973, pp.14f.

6 W.R. Schmidt, ed., *Catalyzing Hope for Justice*, Geneva, WCC, 1986, pp.120f.; cf. M. Kaessmann, *Die eucharistische Vision*, Munich, Kaiser, 1992, p.231.

7 R. Dickinson, *To Set at Liberty the Oppressed*, Geneva, WCC, 1975, p.51.

8 M. Arruda, *Ecumenism and a New World Order*, Geneva, WCC, 1980, p.12.

9 "Service and Unity", statement by CICARWS reprinted in *Midstream*, Vol. 18, 1979, p.175.

10 *An Orthodox Approach to Diaconia*, Geneva, WCC, 1980, p.36.

11 *Ecumenism and a New World Order*, p.44.

12 D. de Gaspar, C. Espiritu and R. Green, eds, *World Hunger: A Christian Reappraisal*, Geneva, WCC, 1982, p.34.

13 *The Churches in Eastern Europe and the Ecumenical Sharing of Resources*, Geneva, WCC, 1983, p.22.

14 J.A. Kudadje and K. Molo, eds, *Towards Abundant Life*, Geneva, WCC, n.d., pp.97, 37.

15 In K. Slack, ed., *Hope in the Desert*, WCC, 1986, p.122.

16 On this sense of powerlessness, see *The Gospel, the Poor and the Churches*, London, Social and Community Planning Research and Christian Aid, 1994.

17 *In Search of a Theology of Development*, Geneva, SODEPAX, 1969, p.152.

18 *Loc. cit.*, p.123.

19 *Political Activities and Campaigning by Charities*, London, HMSO, 1995.

20 J.H. Oldham, ed., *The Churches Survey Their Task*, London, Allen & Unwin, 1937, p.94f.

21 *The Role of the "Diakonia" of the Church in Contemporary Society*, Geneva, WCC, 1966, p.34.

22 *Digest*, p.39.

23 *Uppsala 68 Speaks*, p.47.

24 In *The Ecumenical Review*, Vol. 26, 1974, p.111.

25 *Justice and Mercy*, p.10.

26 D. Preman Niles, comp., *Between the Flood and the Rainbow*, Geneva, WCC, 1992, pp.169f.

27 See P. Gruber, "Interchurch Aid", in *Dictionary of the Ecumenical Movement*, Geneva, WCC, 1991, pp.517f.

28 Cf. already the Amsterdam Assembly Report of 1948, ed. W.A. Visser 't Hooft, Geneva, WCC, 1949, p.75.

29 W.A. Visser 't Hooft, ed., *Evanston Report*, Geneva, WCC, 1955, pp.137f.

30 *Dilemmas and Opportunities*, Geneva, WCC, 1959, p.74.

31 W.A. Visser 't Hooft, ed., *New Delhi Report*, Geneva, WCC, 1962, pp.95, 106f. and 240.

32 *Christians in the Technical and Social Revolutions of Our Time*, p.53.

33 D. Munby, ed., *World Development: Challenge to the Churches*, Geneva, SODEPAX, 1969, pp.16, 9f.

34 *Uppsala 68 Speaks*, pp.45, 51.

35 See J. de Santa Ana, ed., *Towards a Church of the Poor*, p.xv.

36 "Structures of Captivity and Lines of Liberation", *The Ecumenical Review*, Vol. 27, no. 1, 1975, p.44.

37 See *Catalyzing Hope for Justice*, p.28.

38 *Evanston Report*, p.113.
39 *Amsterdam Report* p.77.
40 See *Evanston Report*, p.124.
41 *Uppsala Report*, p.51.
42 See C.I. Itty "Just, Participatory and Sustainable Society", in *Dictionary of the Ecumenical Movement*, p.551.
43 D.M.Paton, ed., *Breaking Barriers*, Geneva, WCC, 1976, p.23.
44 *Ecumenism and a New World Order*, p.18.
45 *Breaking Barriers*, p.124.
46 Cf. Minutes of the Thirtieth Meeting of the WCC Central Committee, 1974, p.44.
47 *Your Kingdom Come*, Geneva, WCC, 1980, p.184.
48 D. Gill, ed., *Gathered for Life*, Geneva, WCC, 1983, p.3.
49 *Called to be Neighbours*, p.124.
50 See M. Kinnamon, ed., *Signs of the Spirit*, Geneva, WCC, 1991, pp.53-66.
51 On this see *Christian Faith and the World Economy Today: A Study Document*, Geneva, WCC, 1992.
52 *Digest*, pp.57, 50f.
53 R.H. Green, ed., *The International Financial System: An Ecumenical Critique*, Geneva, WCC, 1985, pp.66, 86.
54 *Sharing Life*, pp.28f., 38.
55 *Between the Flood and the Rainbow*, p.180.
56 *Signs of the Spirit*, pp.242, 63.
57 *Uppsala 68 Speaks*, p.42.
58 Cf. P. Gruber, *Fetters of Injustice*, pp.55f.
59 *In Search of a Theology of Development*, p.152.
60 "The Economic Threat to Peace", in *The Ecumenical Review*, Vol. 27, no. 1, 1975, p.69.
61 *Christians in the Technical and Social Revolutions of Our Time*, p.49.
62 "Threats to Survival", in *Study Encounter*, Vol. 10, no. 4, 1974, p.10.
63 *Breaking Barriers*, p.123.
64 *Towards a Church in Solidarity with the Poor*, p.3.
65 *Towards a Church of the Poor*, pp.xix, 97-113.
66 P. Abrecht, ed., *Faith and Science in an Unjust World*, Vol. 2, Geneva, WCC, 1980, p.128.
67 *Called to be Neighbours*, p.124.
68 Kudadjie and Molo, *op. cit.*, p.30.

4. "Why Do You Fund Guerrillas?" The Debate about Power

This question on the doorstep had its roots in 1969 when the WCC central committee, meeting in Canterbury, responded to the call of the Uppsala assembly the previous year by setting up the Programme to Combat Racism (PCR). The immediate background was the struggle then going on in South Africa to liberate 20 million people from the oppressive regime of apartheid. It was an overtly racist regime, treating people differently, for better but mostly for very much worse, simply because they were of a different colour. And it made the vast majority a great deal poorer than they would otherwise have been.

PCR was set up to support oppressed racial groups, organizations like the African National Congress (ANC), and the victims of racial oppression: imprisoned, tortured, banned, exiled, bereaved, impoverished, forcibly removed from their homes, denied adequate health care, houses and education. Part of the programme was a Special Fund which made annual grants to such groups.

Those who gave to the Special Fund were not allowed to stipulate who should benefit or in what way. That was a matter of consultation with the oppressed themselves. Those who received the funds had to meet only two requirements: they must represent people suffering racial discrimination; and they must use the money for humanitarian and educational purposes, not to purchase arms.

Christian Aid, along with other ecumenical agencies and many WCC member churches, distanced itself from PCR from the start. Questioned by the media, it made clear that it would not be contributing. While this decision alienated many of its staff and some of its supporters, who saw it as a betrayal of the very people they believed they were called to stand by, it was no doubt designed to reassure the vast majority of donors that their money remained in safe hands and would not be fostering armed revolution or supporting so-called guerrillas (or, to be blunt, black people fighting white governments). Even so, Christian Aid continued for many years to be criticized for the way it did speak out against apartheid and oppression and for the supportive but unfashionable things it had to say about liberation movements in Africa and Central America. It was attacked for trying to put the terrible deeds of some black people in South Africa, such as necklace-killings, in context, setting them alongside the atrocities perpetrated by the apartheid regime and the horrors inflicted on informers and enemies by European resistance movements during the German occupation. The flames of criticism were also fanned when Christian Aid made a gift in kind to the ANC in 1986, providing medicines for South African exiles and local people in Tanzania. It was little compared to the solid support given by other agencies, but in the eyes of some it counted as "funding guerrillas".

PCR had to do with the political dimension of the struggle against poverty, which we discussed in the previous chapter: the need to match immediate help with attempts to confront causes and bring about structural change. But it brought to the fore the even more difficult issue of power. Together they make a heady cocktail for the would-be charitable to swallow.

These two elements were made explicit when the WCC central committee made plans for the programme. First, structural change: the churches were called upon "to move beyond charity, grants and traditional programming to relevant and sacrificial action leading to new relationships of dignity and justice among all men and to become agents for a radical reconstruction of society". Then the issue of power: "There can be no justice in our world without a transfer of economic resources to undergird the redistribution of political power and to make cultural self-determination meaningful... In this transfer of resources a corporate act [i.e., PCR] by the ecumenical fellowship of churches can provide a significant moral lead."[1]

The vocabulary

Power is repeatedly recognized as a key issue in the ecumenical documents. It can be mapped out in terms of three groups of oft-repeated words indicating what is opposed, what is approved of and how change is brought about.

1. What is opposed

The documents are against "paternalistic" and "patronizing" attitudes which assume a superior ability to take care of the needy who cannot take care of themselves. They are against the political and cultural "domination" and "imperialism" which impose their own devices and desires on others, usually under the guise of what is best for them. They are against "dependency" which at best leaves the weaker party at the mercy of the strong and at worst makes them their tool. They are against "donor-recipient" or "handing-down" relationships which assume that the materially better off and the powerful (who are often the same) are the only ones with anything to give.

At the world missionary conference in Edinburgh in 1910, V.A. Azariah of India testified to the "heroism and self-denying labours of the missionary bodies" for which the Indian church would always be grateful: "You have given your goods to feed the poor; you have given your bodies to be burned." But, he added: "We also ask for love. Give us friends." Philip Potter, former general secretary of the WCC, described Azariah's plea, gracious as it was, as the first attack in a world meeting on the relationship of domination and dependence that existed between giving or sending churches and receiving ones, an early call to end paternalism in favour of an attitude of friendship and true partnership. [2]

A conference on "The Development Challenge" organized by SODEPAX in Montreal in 1969 recognized that "the drastic imbalance of power between rich and poor is at the heart of the development problem". It was openly critical of the use of certain words:

> Paternalistic patterns of domination implied by the use of such words as "aid", "technical assistance" and "free transfers" are symptomatic of the continuous tendency of the developed countries to limit or even remove the possibilities of self-determination in the underdeveloped countries. We suggest that use of words which to many have paternalistic and patronizing overtones should be discontinued and that the vocabulary as well as the administration of development co-operation should promote solidarity and mutuality. [3]

The WCC's world mission conference in 1972-73 in Bangkok returned to the theme of domination which Potter noted coming to the fore as early as 1910: "Mission agencies have been, and still are, to a greater or lesser degree involved in this domination." It recommended that the Commission on World Mission and Evangelism (CWME) urge and assist mission agencies

> to examine critically their involvement as part of patterns of political and economic domination, and to re-evaluate the role of personnel and finance at their disposal in the light of that examination... [and] to evaluate critically to what extent and in what ways their patterns of missionary engagement reflect cultural imperialism or involve indiscriminating cultural imposition on churches with which they are related, and what are the consequences for the selfhood, identity and mission of these churches. [4]

The report from a Lutheran World Federation consultation in Nairobi in 1974 acknowledged that paternalism "tends to linger on in new forms" (after formal political independence) but thought that the secular world had tackled it rather better than the churches:

> Whether we like it or not, there is a neo-paternalistic tendency reflected in both aid-criteria and procedures of screening requests and controlling implementation. While donor countries and secular agencies are well on their way to solving these problems, the churches and church-related agencies are rather late in seeking solutions.

The churches "must overcome undesirable attitudes reflected in the distinction between donor and recipient churches". As a result of such attitudes, many decisions were made by those who saw themselves as the "donors", failing to recognize that "we are all donors and recipients at the same time". [5]

When CICARWS, CCPD and CWME came together in 1982 at Glion, Switzerland, to discuss a new way of sharing resources among the churches, they reiterated the belief that the existing structures of giving and receiving (for example, project lists), far from overcoming problems, actually "perpetuate the patterns of domination and dependence between and within the churches". Instead of creating a more just state of affairs, "funds flowing from rich to poor churches are part of the unjust structures of the world". [6]

2. What is approved of

If that is what the documents are against, what do they favour? Here words like "self-reliance" and "independence" come into play. Such terms can themselves be patronizing, of course, if they are heard as suggesting that people, given the opportunity, would in fact be reluctant or unable to take care of themselves. They sound less patronizing when used to insist that the weak should not have to wait on the calculated generosity of the strong, or simply be exploited by them, but should have the freedom to go their own way under their own steam. The vocabulary becomes more thoughtful — and perhaps more conservative — when it goes on to speak about "inter-dependence" rather than dependence, the "mutuality" of giving and receiving, and shared responsibilities. It is true that we are inter-dependent, but this truth can also be pointed out as a way of justifying our not letting go. When the conversation goes further and turns to "equality" it may be in danger of losing touch with reality.

The word most frequently on the lips of the ecumenical family seems to be "partnership". There is a good deal of talk about "partners in mission" and our "partners" in development. Often this refers in a rather revealing way to the organizations and churches of the South and of the poor, who are usually thought of as "receivers" rather than "donors", objects and instruments of development rather than initiators. But if the term "partners" is used only for them, partnership carries the flavour of a secondary role. All this reminds us that equal partnership remains an aspiration and not an achievement. We have to learn to use the word more carefully, to watch our language.

The International Missionary Council (IMC) was already using the word "partnership" in 1947 at its meeting in Whitby, Ontario, Canada, on "The Witness of a Revolutionary Church". "Real partnership", it believed

> involves the grace of receiving as well as the grace of giving. Within the partnership there is no reason why churches which are economically weak should hesitate to receive help from those which are economically strong. It is taken for granted that no Christian body will try to take advantage of its financial strength to secure dominance over any other. [7]

The quotation offers a delightful mixture of naiveté (that no Christian body would misuse its strength) and common sense (that in some matters, especially financial, some have little if anything to offer but the readiness to receive). It could also allude to the way in which givers and receivers need each other if anything is to be achieved. Overall, it seems designed to reassure the receivers rather than establish partnership as an entirely mutual relationship in which both give and both receive.

The emphasis was different in the report of the Division of Inter-Church Aid and Service to Refugees to the WCC central committee in 1955: "All churches in all countries should be giving churches, although the giving may take many forms. This requires a worldwide programme in which all churches may participate on an equal footing."[8] The same emphasis shines through the report of the 1959 WCC conference in Thessalonica on Christian Action in Rapid Social Change, half of whose participants came from Asia, Africa and Latin America: "All peoples have a part to play in the development of the world. Those who have the resources and the skill can help others to develop. But they can only do this if they realize that all men have gifts to contribute."[9]

The New Delhi assembly of 1961 again sounded the note of mutuality:

> The static distinction of "receiving church" and "giving church" must go so that all will share spiritual, material and personal gifts in the light of the total economy of the household of God... Aid can never be and should not be a one-way affair. Out of their rich cultural heritage, the developing nations have much to contribute to the enrichment of the life of the people of the world as a whole.[10]

The Commission on World Mission and Evangelism, meeting in Mexico City in 1963, returned to the idea of partnership in mission as it worked on the theme "Witness in Six Continents". Mission is not merely from the West to the South. It is mutual. It moves in all directions including South to West. It is *world* mission not *Western* mission, in which all the churches are equal partners and join in common missionary actions.[11]

Leslie Cooke linked partnership with equality at the DICARWS world consultation in Swanwick in 1966: "We cannot move forward into a real community except on the basis of partnership in a common purpose of churches who recognize one another as of equal status in the same ecumenical fellowship."[12]

A joint WCC and Roman Catholic conference in Beirut in 1968 spoke against dependence in favour of inter-dependence:

> The issues of social and international justice are not those of charity and almsgiving, of patrons and dependents. The Christian vision is one of profound inter-dependence, of shared experience and support, of man-

kind working jointly at its own development and achieving together "the glorious liberty of the sons of God". [13]

Years later, in 1980, an international working group on the ecumenical sharing of resources, meeting in Geneva, expressed this equality in the symbol of "empty hands", where people meet with hands full of gifts for each other but must empty them if they are to embrace and receive from each other. The study guide they produced, which took *Empty Hands* as its title, was "an invitation to join in the vulnerable and risky task of sharing with empty hands. Central to this vision was that we are all receivers." [14]

When a new resource-sharing system was approved by the WCC central committee in 1982, the proposal insisted that

> the transfer of funds should take place within a framework of equality and trust relationships based on a common understanding of objectives and priorities. Sharing of resources is a mutual process which requires transparency on all sides. [15]

3. How change is brought about

But if the order of the day — and of the kingdom — is genuine partnership, mutuality and equality (less is said about independence and self-reliance), how are they to come about? How is the crucial shift away from overbearing paternalism and dependency to be achieved? The answer according to the documents lies in words like "empowerment", "shared decision-making" and "participation". They are all echoed in the proposals for resource-sharing made in 1982: "It involves participation and sharing of decision-making. The partners should be accountable to each other about their decisions, their criteria for using and raising funds, their priorities and the way they exercise power." [16]

Since these terms assume such importance, it is worthwhile to listen to them one by one.

a. Power and empowerment. The world conference on Church and Society in 1966 was, as we have seen, divided in its approach to change. Nevertheless, it faithfully recorded how the active and in-fluential groups in the Third World often saw the need to revolutionize

> the structures of power if there is to be any improvement in the situation of those people who suffer because of the existing system. They reject the

view of many in the industrialized nations that if economic development occurs rapidly enough, changes in the structures of power will be a natural by-product.

They believed the reverse was true. Empowerment had to come first. [17]

The WCC assembly in Uppsala in 1968 saw power as a priority issue for mission: "For the sake of the new humanity the powerless must exercise power." [18] The next year the international consultation in Notting Hill which set up the Programme to Combat Racism claimed that the question of economic, social and political power is basic to the problem of development. Equality based on power is the *sine qua non* for worldwide justice. The report of the SODEPAX conference the same year spoke in similar terms:

> The drastic imbalance of power between rich and poor is at the heart of the development problem... Both the domination of the underdeveloped countries by the developed and the mutuality of the process of development make necessary the confrontation between those without power and those with power and the confrontation of both with the insights of the gospel's commitment to a more just and human order. These things we regard as the essence of the work of SODEPAX. [19]

A 1973 memorandum from the Council of the Evangelical Church in Germany acknowledged that "an appropriate change in the power structures may... become a prerequisite of the establishment of greater justice". [20] CICARWS, commending a 1981 report on the use and abuse of food aid, agreed: "At the end of the day, we are talking about power." [21] A world consultation on diakonia in Geneva in 1982 put the empowerment of the people before participation and decision-making: without it they could never really determine what happened in order to remedy their situation. [22] In 1983 the WCC assembly at Vancouver committed itself to work for the sharing of power, both in a new international economic order and in the church. [23] El Escorial followed this up in 1987 with a commitment from the participants to work towards the empowerment of people: "to enable people to organize themselves and realize their potential and power as individuals and communities, working towards the kind of self-reliance and self-determination which are an essential condition of interdependence". [24]

Christian Aid took up much the same theme when it adopted a statement of commitment in the same year. Its title, "To Strengthen the Poor", clearly indicated its underlying concern. Two of its summary paragraphs went like this:

> The world, we believe, is likely to be a fairer place where strength is not left to take advantage of weakness but is balanced by strength... We must act strategically to strengthen the arm of the poor until they can stand up to those who so often act against them, and have the power to determine their own development under God.

Many other Northern agencies have spoken the language of empowerment as well.

And so, by the 1990s, ecumenical gatherings have come to refer to the issue of power almost as a matter of course. The WCC assembly in Canberra in 1991 is an example: its report speaks more than once about the sharing of power. [25] The Australian Council of Churches' Commission for World Christian Action is another. Its guiding principles, adopted in 1993, state: "Partnership means that we work for *change in power structures* and in so doing empower those in Australia [no doubt Aboriginal peoples] for creative change, and that we do not disempower our partners through creating or continuing dependency." [26]

b. Participation. CCPD made this a watchword almost from the very beginning. Its emphasis on "people's participation" was meant to underline that the poor and oppressed are not the objects of development (in which case they only pay the price of it) but its main agents. They are the subjects of history. It is they who bring justice about, not the rich and powerful, who are unlikely either to change significantly their attitudes or relinquish their privileges. The rich are not to be called upon to bring about justice and a better life for the poor through economic growth or anything else. It is the poor themselves, working with one another in solidarity, who will bring it about.

"What we have learned", wrote the CCPD commission when it met in Albano, Italy, in 1973, only three years after it was set up,

> is that there is another programme style, based on people's participation and organization, by which the poor become agents of their own development, identifying their needs, mobilizing their resources, shaping their future, and in which input resources from beyond is the complementary enabler. [27]

This sounds less like being empowered than realizing the power you already possess or, as CCPD put it following a second consultation with CICARWS in Montreux in 1974, "the mobilization of the power of the poor and oppressed". [28] Similar ideas were expressed in a 1979 CCPD meeting in Yaoundé, Cameroon. The poor are not

to be considered as objects of "poverty policies" which were and still are elaborated without their involvement... The purpose of work for liberation is to create awareness and power in the people so that they can become the subject of change for the kind of society they want to live in. [29]

"The poor" and "the people" are not of course a single category. They too include their own powerful groups and social strata.

c. Decision-making. This is the most frequently mentioned practical outcome of "empowerment" and "participation". Decisions in future are to be taken elsewhere, or taken in consultation with those who are being decided about, or made by those who previously had no say in them at all.

Many if not most of the decisions are about money. After noting that "the heart of the problem is one of power", the committee on Ecumenical Sharing of Personnel (ESP) went on to say at a meeting in Choully, near Geneva, in 1972 that

money is the symbol of this power. Traditionally, those who have the money make the decisions about the projects on which it will be spent and the personnel who will work on the projects. The ESP committee is concerned to shift power from the powerful to the powerless. It, therefore, looks first for a means of transferring money to the poorer churches before basic decisions are made about who should be employed to work on particular projects. [30]

Many of those decisions were in the hands of the funding agencies. "They can choose both the type of project they want to support and the area of interest where they want to place their aid." [31] They still can. The German agency EZE, setting out its programme priorities in 1984, seemed to agree that this should change:

The responsibility for each programme supported by EZE lies with the respective partner organization overseas. It has to decide on the concept, the approach and the implementation of the programme, as it has also to bear the risks and the consequences arising out of it.

The need for the poor to influence decisions is a constant theme in the ecumenical documents. "We need international decision-making structures within which the poor can have countervailing power" (Jan Pronk). [32] "At every level of the decision-making process where the methods, goals and size of aid programmes are determined, Christian and secular representatives of the Third World should also have a voice" (Council of the Evangelical Church in Germany). [33] "The practice of solidarity... consequently implies shared decision-making. The choice of projects, decisions as to the use and allocation of resources have to be shared and the appropriate decision-making processes have to be devised" (Jean Fischer). [34] "God has given to all people the right and power of decision-making. The deprival of that power... is a major cause of the distortions of production and distribution in the world economy of today" (Church and Society conference, 1979). [35] "People should participate in the decisions which affect them so that they can determine for themselves the appropriate directions" (Consultation on Resource Sharing, 1982). [36] "Economic and social structures which perpetuate inequality and poverty must be replaced by a new international economic order and political structure which ensures the full participation of all people in the decisions which affect their lives" (Larnaca, 1986). [37] "If we cannot easily forgo the power that is tied to the money we collect, we must at least find ways to make the weak strong... They must decide about the allocation and use of resources as well as receive them" (Christian Aid, *To Strengthen the Poor*, 1987). The participants at El Escorial committed themselves to "a new understanding of sharing in which those who have been marginalized [not only the poor, but also women and young people]... take their place at the centre of all decisions and actions as equal partners". [38] "The poor should gain access to goods and services as well as the means to influence all the decisions which affect their lives" (ICCO, 1994). [39]

The ecumenical documents do not offer a great deal of analysis of some of the constraints on participation, such as those imposed by culture, powerful "leaders" and social groups, or of the various levels of participation, which range from information-sharing and consultation to cooperation and genuine initiatives by "the people". [40]

d. A summary. Having looked at the vocabulary used by the ecumenical family to discuss the issue of power, we can now summarize the issue itself quite briefly in general terms. Poverty is less about a lack of resources than about their unfair distribution. It is the bitter fruit of injustice. Injustice arises when there is an imbalance of power. The weak become over-dependent on the strong. The strong, acting in their own self-interest, patronize, dominate and exploit the weak. The answer is not the charity of donors, however generous, but a better balance of power. All people need some chance, perhaps an equal chance, to influence the decisions that affect their lives and to resist those who will otherwise take decisions which are not in their favour. It is in such a balance, and not in fine words or good intentions, that the seeds of mutuality and partnership lie.

Although the language used is often the same, there are two rather different areas in which the issue of power has to be tackled. One is the secular world, which includes everyone. The other is the church. Understandably, perhaps, the ecumenical documents have a good deal more to say about the second than the first, since the main actors are churches, councils of churches and church-related agencies. [41]

Power in the secular world

There are plenty of references in the ecumenical documents to unjust structures and the need to change them. The trading system, for example, should be made more fair. There should be more opportunities for Third World countries to manufacture and sell their products, enjoy fairer prices and improved wages and working conditions. The banking system should be made more fair. There should be more favourable interest rates, longer-term loans and debt forgiveness. But these proposals, admirable as they may be, usually sound more like appeals to the better nature of the strong than attempts to shift the balance of power towards those whose position is weak because the market is unprofitable for them and they are burdened with debts they cannot repay.

When the tougher issue of power is raised, it is still only in very general terms. Concrete suggestions are few and far between. For example, the 1958 consultation in Odense on European responsibilities to Africa and Asia recognized the effects of European trading policies on developing countries but did little more than warn about the dangers of paternalism and demand "common partnership".[42] The Geneva conference on Church and Society in 1966 also talked about partnership: it saw the urgent need in developing countries "to replace economic paternalism or domination by economic partnership among all nations". The aim, however, had more to do with treating poorer countries with respect than with giving them power. The churches

> should condemn relationships between donors and recipients that are inconsistent with human dignity and a biblical doctrine of creation... The spirit in which technical aid is given and the cooperation of the host country are fully as important as its amount... The self-respect of developing nations demands that development be seen as a joint or cooperative effort based on mutual interest rather than paternalism or charity.

The Geneva conference did speak about changes in the structures of power, though as we have seen it tended to speak with two voices. One, largely of the West, believed such changes would follow in the train of economic development. The other, largely of the Third World, believed structural change had to come first. Exactly how would depend on the context: "while in one situation revolutionary change may be necessary, in another more evolutionary methods may be appropriate".[43]

CCPD has probably struggled more consistently than most members of the ecumenical family with how in concrete terms the poor are to be empowered and shifts in the balances of power brought about:

> This process of empowering the powerless to become the subjects of change occurs mainly through helping them organize themselves to face immediate local power structures. Such conflicts and confrontations in the micro-level help people become conscientized and organized to deal with major issues on a larger scale.

Communication links within countries and regions and around the world are also important, so that people's movements and organizations can be in touch, share their experiences, give and receive support and develop common strategies.[44]

The importance of organizing was also recognized by Christian Aid when it enumerated ways in which the poor can be strengthened. The point was somewhat overlaid (perhaps in order to avoid sounding too "political"), but it is there: if the poor

are well nourished and in good health..., if they have land..., if they can
earn a living and have a measure of financial independence..., if they are
self-reliant and self-sufficient..., if they are knowledgeable about the
causes of their poverty..., if they are protected by just laws, they are
stronger. If they are organized to cooperate and act together, they are
stronger.[45]

And there are endless stories of the landless of Asia, of the forest-
dwellers and the *favelas* of Latin America, of trade unions in the
Caribbean, of co-operatives in Africa, of people's movements in the
Philippines — all of them organizing themselves to confront the
powers that be.

Little is ever said about armed struggle; and if the ecumenical
family has shown some sympathy and understanding for the resort to
arms in certain circumstances, it has studiously avoided giving financial support to it. The Programme to Combat Racism, as we have
seen, put down as one of its two conditions that funds should be used
for humanitarian and educational purposes, not for the purchase of
arms. In 1971 the WCC central committee did discuss whether
organizations of racially oppressed people involved in the use of
violence should be supported.[46] Further discussions on "Violence,
Non-Violence and the Struggle for Social Justice" followed.[47] In 1987
against the background of Northern Ireland as well as the struggles of
the poor in the Third World, Christian Aid had this to say:

> There are those in today's world who feel that one way to strengthen the
> poor is to supply them with arms. Christian Aid could never take such a
> step and has never done so. Quite apart from our status as a charity, many
> among us, including some who themselves suffer at the hands of
> violence, regard it as counter-productive and quite contrary to the gospel.
> We acknowledge that there are Christians who believe that in carefully
> defined circumstances armed resistance is justified. Where the poor
> conclude that is the only way for them to take, we respect their decision
> even where we disagree with it and certainly cannot support it.[48]

In recent years a number of factors, including the collapse of state-
centred socialism in Eastern Europe, the resulting "crisis for the Left",
the growing influence and "success" of free-market capitalism and the
perceived retreat of oppression in a number of countries, most notably
in South Africa but also in Latin America, have led to rather different
proposals as to how in practice to deal with the issue of power. One is

by increasing the power of poor people in the marketplace with affordable credit, good information, protection from extortion, better marketing services and the like. Another is by promoting participation through civil society, democracy (often as a condition of aid) and better representation of poorer countries in such international institutions as the UN, the World Trade Organization, the World Bank and the International Monetary Fund. Human rights are also much discussed. "One of the classic human rights," according to the Dutch agency ICCO in *Signs of Hope*, is "the right to participate in decision-making processes."

Power in the church

When it comes to the church, many schemes for dealing with the issue of power have been worked out by the ecumenical family. Some are quite closely interrelated and can be grouped under three headings: (1) putting a stop to it all; (2) "no questions asked"; and (3) ecumenical sharing of decisions.

1. Putting a stop to it all

The idea of a "moratorium" on the flow of resources from Northern churches and agencies to the South was designed to deal with dependency. If these were simply cut off, it would greatly reduce the influence of the Northern churches and agencies and make the younger churches and partner organizations stronger and more independent, calling their own tune rather than dancing to somebody else's. It would force them to stand on their own feet.

The moratorium was debated more in relation to missions than to aid and development. It was mooted, though not under that name, as early as 1938 at the conference of the International Missionary Council in Tambaram, India.[49] In 1971, Emerito Nacpil of the Philippines called for a moratorium on missionaries, arguing that after the child is born, the midwife is no longer needed. Any continuing partnership could only be

> between the weak and the strong. And that means the continued dependence of the weak upon the strong and the continued dominance of the strong over the weak, notwithstanding our efforts and protestations to the contrary... The most *missionary* service a missionary under the present system can do today in Asia is to go home! And the most free and vital

and daring act the younger churches can do today is to stop asking for missionaries under the present system.[50]

In the same year John Gatu of Kenya issued a similar challenge, and not for the first time: "We in the Third World must liberate ourselves from the bondage of Western dependency by refusing anything that renders impotent the development of our spiritual resources." José Míguez Bonino of Argentina followed suit: "We in the younger churches have to learn the discipline of freedom to accept and freedom to refuse... You [in the older 'sending' churches] have to learn to renounce resources as a means of domination. In order to do this you must learn to lose control over what you give".[51]

A moratorium on personnel and funds was considered sympathetically by the committee on Ecumenical Sharing of Personnel in 1972, and by the WCC's world mission conference in Bangkok the same year. At the assembly of the All Africa Conference of Churches in Lusaka in 1974, a moratorium was described "as the most viable means of giving the African church the power to perform its mission in the African context, as well as to lead our governments and peoples in finding solutions to economic and social dependency".[52] The idea was the subject of a consultation in Geneva in 1975 and was debated later that year at the WCC assembly in Nairobi. It "is not a slamming of the door in the brother's face; it is a dynamic process seeking a new way", overcoming the existing patterns of domination and dependence.[53] But it was never put into practice and little was subsequently heard of it. Jan Pronk of the Netherlands, addressing the CICARWS-CCPD consultation in Montreux in 1974, probably hit the nail on the head when he surmised that in terms of self-reliance what would be more relevant than a moratorium on aid would be "a moratorium on the ongoing creeping process of strengthening the internal decision-making structures of the rich".[54]

2. "No questions asked"

Priority projects and unearmarked grants were designed to give the South far more say in how money was spent.

CICARWS began to establish what were called regional groups in 1972. They were in the South, not in the North. "Regions" for the most part meant "continents". The groups screened and listed projects for funding. In the case of priority projects, the funding was virtually guaranteed. Their priority was decided by their originators in the South and respected by the funding agencies. When WCC project lists were reviewed in 1987 and again in the early 1990s and largely phased out, these priority projects were retained to reflect a continuing determination "that decision-making must be transferred to the areas where the needs arise and are identified". [55]

The practice of making unearmarked grants was rejected at first by donor agencies but grew as time went on. A consultation organized by CICARWS in 1978 believed "that non-earmarked contributions will help the churches to express their real needs instead of seeking to meet the requirements of the funding agencies". [56] The working group on the ecumenical sharing of resources, meeting in Geneva in 1980, explicitly discussed unearmarked grants in the context of power. It named block grants and undesignated giving as expressions of confidence in each other and of solidarity. [57]

More radical voices in the South claimed that these resources now being shared by the ecumenical family were theirs by right, and challenged the North to hand over far more of them, without condition and with no questions asked. That challenge was never taken up — and this was long before so-called "back-donors" in the North, including governments, began to be increasingly concerned about monitoring their grants and the impact of the programmes they were funding. In 1977 and 1979 ICCO in the Netherlands organized a "reverse consortium", at which representatives from the South discussed ICCO's work instead of the other way round. The consortium judged that it was not feasible and not desirable to transfer authority over the assignment of funds to the partners. Despite some small project funds being set up in the South, this judgment has not been noticeably reversed.

But some ecumenical organizations did act differently. The Ecumenical Church Loan Fund, founded in 1946, the programme on Ecumenical Sharing of Personnel set up after the 1968 WCC assembly, the Ecumenical Development Fund established by CCPD in 1970 and the Ecumenical Development Cooperative Society founded in 1975 by the WCC and the Council of Churches in the Netherlands endeavoured to share not only resources but also power, putting decisions about funds and the deployment of people firmly into the hands of their partners in the developing countries.

3. The ecumenical sharing of decisions

Regionalization as a way of sharing decisions was born at Larnaca in 1986 — or rather "born again", since the term was not a new one. In essence this was a call for more decisions to be made regionally and locally and by local people. As early as 1971 DICARWS had talked about giving far more responsibility to the regions in the administration of the project list;[58] and in 1979 CICARWS wished to include in the same process responsibility for country programmes and personnel as well as projects.[59]

Regionalization was taken up into the debate about the ecumenical sharing of resources which had been on the WCC's agenda since 1976, when the central committee inaugurated a study programme on resource-sharing in the wake of the moratorium debate.[60] Regionalization won the commitment of those who took part in the El Escorial consultation in 1987, and of a meeting of the heads of agencies in 1989. Round table structures, earlier called "consortia", were established in 1984 as a way of sharing resources at the national rather than regional level. Before them came country programmes, started as an experiment by CICARWS in 1976, which brought the churches in a country together to decide on a programme and how much of it they could support themselves before looking for outside funding. "Country policy papers" are the more recent children of the agencies. They are drawn up after consultation between Northern agencies and Southern partners, often at a so-called "partners meeting".

Just as all of these devices are relevant to the attempt to be more strategic (see Chapter 3), so they are all relevant to the issue of power. All of them look to a similar format for sharing decisions about the use of resources: they bring the interested parties around one table; they reach agreement about what needs to be done; they set it out in the form of policy statements, guidelines and priorities; and they commit all concerned to honour those agreements in any subsequent "sharing of resources" (which still means mostly funding), through whatever channels.

Ways of working established by other ecumenical groups such as the Evangelical Community for Apostolic Action (CEVAA) in 1971, the Council for World Mission in 1977 and the Interchurch Fund for International Development look very similar.[61] The approach might be called the Ecumenical Sharing of Decisions.

A careful if not very elegant statement about regionalization called "Regionalized Decision-Making" was agreed to in 1993 by a meeting of representatives of the WCC, national and regional ecumenical bodies, regional groups and agencies. Later the same year it was agreed to implement its recommendations for an experimental period of three years. The statement talks mainly about regional groups and round tables, but it has a wider reference and illustrates what the ecumenical sharing of decisions means in practice.

First, it must include all the interested parties:

> Regional groups should include representatives of churches in the region, Northern agencies, regional ecumenical organizations, Unit IV (of the WCC), mission boards and ecumenical networks and movements. They may also include representatives of non-church-related movements... They should be inclusive in representation of women, youth and marginalized groups.

Everyone must now have a say.

Second, it must make decisions which really make a difference, providing "specific guidelines and priorities for action in the region". Only if it is "seen to be making a real difference in the lives of people in their region" will it be credible.

Third, there must be transparency, especially on the side of the agencies, as to what powers they do and do not bring to the table: "Agencies agreed to... state clearly what they believe they could and could not do — knowing they may well be challenged."

Fourth, the ecumenical sharing of decisions involves a commitment to abide by the decisions made:

> Accepting guidance of the regional groups on issues, priorities and criteria for funding; making... commitments to reflect the priorities and criteria set by the regional groups...; being accountable and providing clear, specific reports to one another about such acceptance and commitments.

If agreements were not kept the parties to them should at least return to the table and hear why.

The meeting looked forward to a growing sense of "ecumenical discipline" ensuring that these commitments would be respected.

Realism

We have looked at the issue of power by looking first at the vocabulary used by the ecumenical family to talk about it in general, and then at some of the practical steps which have been taken, especially within the church. In conclusion we need to talk about realism.

At many points the ecumenical documents strike the right note, if only in recognizing that nothing much is going to improve for the poor unless the imbalance of power in the world is confronted and changed. At other points, however, the story is less reassuring. There are, for example, many dreams and visions about sharing power and resources in partnerships of equality: where all are equally the owners or stewards of the earth's resources; where all have an equal say in what happens to them; where all are receivers and givers alike, as much in need as they are well placed to help; where non-material gifts out of a people's culture or character or spirituality are just as important and desirable as material ones; where all are given equal respect and taken with equal seriousness; where those who hold the purse strings count for no more than those who do not.

But along with these dreams come repeated confessions that the dreams have not been fulfilled: that the issue of power has not been confronted; that partnership remains an empty slogan; that words are not matched by deeds; that despite all the fine proposals the actual dynamics between North and South, funding agencies and receiving "partners" remain much the same; that financial considerations all too easily dominate round table discussions and attempts to make shared decisions.

Visions unrealized can be useful for stimulating the continuing prophetic challenge to be self-critical and to go beyond our present ambiguous achievements. They can help to rehearse and recall the sensitivities involved in forging relationships between North and South, agencies and councils of churches, those with money and those without. Visions are not so fine once they cease to relate, however critically, to the reality on the ground, thus obscuring it rather than dealing with it. For whatever ought to be the case, the fact is that the relationships in question are not equal. Power is rarely handed over. Money is decisive. Many "partnerships" might hardly exist at all or attract much interest if money were not involved. And because money plays such a crucial role, much of the power remains with the "donors" who have funds to grant or to withhold.

Perhaps the rhetoric — or "myth", as it has sometimes been called — should be set aside in favour of honest but straightforward deals which meet the interests of both parties. If the life of the organizations of the poor depends on obtaining financial resources, the life of funding agencies increasingly depends on being able to spend money in effective and accountable ways. Both parties could respect the needs of the other. Both could be motivated to make compromises which allow businesslike deals to be struck. Neither need pretend they amount to very much else. Something of that mood can be detected in the report of a consultation on partnership between representatives of national councils of churches and agencies in 1994. Despite some careful language, it is realistic about the power of the North to insist on how other people should go about their development. It recognizes "new geo-political realities and a neo-liberal economic system". It accepts that councils of churches in the South must adopt alien approaches to management and accounting if funds are to be made available:

> This means that organizations and programmes need to be managed professionally and that competent and qualified staff must be adequately equipped and given the necessary integrity to perform well. They [councils of churches] further recognized that the funds involved must be spent according to the purposes they were raised for and must be accounted for in a spirit of mutual transparency. [62]

In other words, an unwelcome deal is struck for the sake of getting things done.

But realism raises another question: are we not devoting disproportionate time and energy in the name of "partnership" to sorting out the power relations and structures of the church when the real issue is the power structures of the world? Are we fiddling while Rome burns? When the world mission conference in Bangkok in 1972 admitted that "partnership in mission remains an empty slogan", it went on to say:

> The power relationships between mission agencies in Europe, North America and Australasia and the churches in other areas to which they relate reflect the economic inequalities between the nations concerned. This is one reason — though not the primary one — why mission

agencies must see the struggle for international economic justice as one of their urgent tasks today. [63]

The reflection within the church of international economic realities is in fact only a tiny reflection, since the resources available to the ecumenical family, which talks so much about resource-sharing, are minuscule compared to the resources of governments, transnational corporations and international financial institutions. The balance of power within the church will in all likelihood be changed only when it comes to reflect a different balance in the world. Realism thus suggests that worldly power is the main issue to tackle and that the ecumenical sharing of resources should refer far more to the resources of the whole ecumenical world than to the resources of the whole ecumenical church.

Time spent on reforming the church is sometimes justified on the ground that the church must have integrity and be true to itself. But this argument is not so convincing if the circumstances in which the church tries to reform itself — in this case the imbalance of power and resources in the world — amount to overwhelming odds. It may be better to admit defeat and try a different strategy. Reforming the church is also commended from time to time as a way of setting an example to the world. It becomes a model of how the world should live — in this instance as a sharing community. This too sounds less convincing if the example is almost impossible to set or if the world is unwilling to be impressed.

If the ecumenical family is to struggle at all for the redistribution of resources within itself and for the justice and independence and equality that go with it, it should perhaps do so with a much more limited but clear-eyed purpose. It should use its resource-sharing systems to strengthen those organizations and agencies in North and South which take a realistic view of how power can actually be shifted, not so much within the church as within the world at large, and which are prepared to organize themselves and bend their energies to bring that shift about.

Finally, while the ecumenical documents often adopt what might be called a theological tone when dealing with the issue of sharing power, one misses a rigorously worked-out Christian theory or theology of power. Such a theology needs to engage with the downside of human nature and its persistence. It needs to come to terms with human insecurity, which clings so tenaciously to power once it gets hold of it. It needs to use this knowledge to undergird and firmly shape the way in which the ecumenical family talks about power and makes practical moves to share it.

Such a theology is not entirely absent from the documents. For example, the section on "Mission and Power" in a 1979 Urban Rural Mission paper, having accepted that power is not evil in itself and can be used for good or ill, recognizes both the necessity and ambiguity of empowering the poor:

> We are very much aware of this demonic character of power when we advocate building power as a means to emancipate the poor. Yet we also believe that every person and every community needs power in order to live in just relationships with other people and communities and that empowerment of those lacking power can be one of the signs of the kingdom of God. [64]

If a rigorous theology of power were more consistently deployed by the ecumenical family, and if it were firmly recognized that the sinful egoist in each of us is too frightened to share power, let alone hand it over, it might help to supply the realism needed to toughen and complement ecumenical visions and to understand why power between the churches is so hard to shift or share. Were the same theology to be disseminated, popularized, appreciated and understood more widely, it might help the questioner on the doorstep to come to terms with "funding guerrillas" and the need to add to the strength of those within and beyond the churches who might one day grow strong enough to challenge the existing order and create a balance of power more in their favour.

NOTES

[1] Minutes of the central committee meeting, 1969, p.273.
[2] See *Empty Hands*, Geneva, WCC, 1980, p.49.
[3] *The Development Challenge*, Geneva, SODEPAX, 1969, p.15.
[4] Minutes of the Bangkok assembly, Geneva, WCC, 1973, pp.22,25.
[5] *Proclamation and Human Development*, Geneva, LWF, 1975, pp.16f.,127.
[6] *Towards a New System of Sharing*, Geneva, WCC, 1983, p.19.
[7] *The Witness of the Revolutionary Church*, London, IMC, 1947, p.24.

[8] Minutes of the central committee meeting, 1955, p.95.

[9] *Dilemmas and Opportunities*, Geneva, WCC, 1959, p.75.

[10] W.A. Visser 't Hooft, ed., *New Delhi Report*, Geneva, WCC, 1962, pp.113, 276.

[11] See B. Carr, "The Moratorium", *National Christian Council Review*, Vol. 95, no. 2, 1975, pp.84f.

[12] *Digest of the 1966 World Consultation on Inter-Church Aid*, Geneva, WCC, 1966, p.130.

[13] D. Munby, ed., *World Development: Challenge to the Churches*, Geneva, SODEPAX, 1969, p.33.

[14] H. van Beek, "Ecumenical Sharing of Resources: Reading the Past to Discern the Future", *The Ecumenical Review*, Vol. 38, 1986, p.444.

[15] *Resource Sharing System*, Geneva, WCC, 1983, pp.15f.

[16] *Ibid.*

[17] *Christians in the Technical and Social Revolutions of Our Time*, Geneva, WCC, 1967, p.141.

[18] N. Goodall, ed., *Uppsala 68 Speaks*, Geneva, WCC, 1968, p.31.

[19] *The Development Challenge*, p.15.

[20] "The Church's Service to Development", *The Ecumenical Review*, Vol. 26, 1974, p.114.

[21] J. Fryer, *Food for Thought*, Geneva, WCC, 1981, p.11.

[22] See *Contemporary Understanding of Diakonia*, Geneva, WCC, 1983, p.4.

[23] See D. Gill, ed., *Gathered for Life*, Geneva, WCC, 1983, p.3.

[24] H. van Beek, ed., *Sharing Life*, Geneva, WCC, 1989, p.29.

[25] See M. Kinnamon, ed., *Signs of the Spirit*, Geneva, WCC, 1991, pp.102, 246, 252.

[26] *The Story of the Commission for World Christian Action*, Sydney, ACC, 1993, p.6.

[27] J. de Santa Ana, ed., *Good News to the Poor*, WCC, 1977, p.111.

[28] Cf. M. Robra, *Ökumenische Sozialethik*, Gütersloh, 1994, p.98.

[29] *Towards a Church in Solidarity with the Poor*, Geneva, WCC, 1980, pp.15, 29.

[30] J. Rossel, "The Mission of the Expatriate", *International Review of Mission*, Vol. 62, 1973, p.477.

[31] *Digest*, p.28.

[32] J. Pronk, "Development in the '70s: Seven Proposals", *The Ecumenical Review*, Vol. 27, 1975, p.23.

[33] "The Church's Service to Development", *loc. cit.*, p.112.

[34] Minutes of the CICARWS commission meeting, 1979, Appendix I, p.38.

[35] P. Abrecht, ed., *Faith and Science in an Unjust World*, Vol. 2, Geneva, WCC, 1980, p.128.

[36] *Towards a New System of Sharing*, p.20.

[37] K. Poser, ed., *Called to be Neighbours*, Geneva, WCC, 1987, p.124.

[38] *Sharing Life*, p.28.

[39] *Signs of Hope*, ICCO, 1994.

[40] Cf. *People's Participation, NGOs and the Flood Action Plan: An Independent Review*, Oxfam-Bangladesh, 1992, pp.22-33.

[41] There is a lengthy section mainly about secular power in the Nairobi assembly report, *Breaking Barriers*, ed. D.M. Paton, Geneva, WCC, 1976, pp.129-33.

[42] *Dilemmas and Opportunities*, p.74.

[43] *Christians in the Technical and Social Revolutions of Our Time*, pp.88, 87, 138f., 143.

[44] *Towards a Church in Solidarity with the Poor*, p.29.

[45] *To Strengthen the Poor*, London, Christian Aid, 1987.

[46] Minutes of the 1971 central committee meeting, p.52.
[47] See *The Ecumenical Review*, Vol. 25, no. 4, 1973, p.430.
[48] *To Strengthen the Poor*.
[49] See K.S. Latourette, in R. Rouse and S.C. Neill, eds, *A History of the Ecumenical Movement*, Vol. 1, p.370.
[50] "Mission but not Missionaries", *IDOC International*, Vol. 63, 1974, pp.79f.
[51] "Missionary, Go Home", *ibid.*, p.72; and "The Present Crisis in Mission", *ibid.*, pp.77f.
[52] "The Moratorium", *ibid.*, p.91.
[53] "Ecumenical Sharing of Personnel", *ibid.*, pp.44f.
[54] "Development in the '70s", *loc. cit.*, p.23.
[55] See T.F. Best, ed., *Vancouver to Canberra: 1983-1990*, Geneva, WCC, 1990, p.177.
[56] *An Orthodox Approach to Diakonia*, Geneva, WCC, 1980, p.14.
[57] See *Empty Hands*, p.25.
[58] Minutes of the 1971 central committee meeting, pp.60f.
[59] See "Towards a New Process for Mission and Service", report for the CICARWS commission, 1979, p.5.
[60] See *Empty Hands*, p.4; *Sharing Life*, p.106.
[61] See "Towards a New System for Sharing: Interview with H. van Beek", *International Review of Mission*, Vol. 73, 1981, p.216.
[62] Report of the Consultation on Partnership Between NCCs and Agencies, Geneva, WCC, 1994.
[63] Minutes of the Bangkok assembly, p.104; cf. *Empty Hands*, p.53.
[64] L. Howell, *People are the Subject*, Geneva, WCC, 1980, p.77.

5. "Are You Oxfam with Hymns?" The Debate about Christian Identity

The title of this chapter reflects another long-running issue in the ecumenical response to poverty. It is sometimes a critical question, especially when it comes from those who believe Christian aid agencies should be actively evangelizing and promoting Christianity. The force of the question then becomes: "What more do you offer than Oxfam with hymns?" Have you nothing more to say to people than the other agencies? We are back to the debate about mission and development.

But even when the question reflects curiosity or perplexity rather than hostility it can be challenging and unsettling. It asks about the difference between "Christian" aid and "secular" or "humanitarian" aid, and whether the difference really amounts to very much. Christian aid agencies surely end up behaving in much the same ways as any other aid agency (and some questioners, especially those who do not like missionaries, would add, "thank goodness!"). They simply deck out what they do with biblical texts and theological language and spiritual songs. At most, as I have heard it said, it is like dressing on the salad, adding a bit of flavour but not greatly affecting the substance.

Of the many attempts in the ecumenical documents of the last fifty years to relate Christian faith to the struggle against poverty, three in particular stand out; and a brief look at them may equip us to answer the question about "Oxfam with hymns". The first attempt was made by CCPD, the second by CICARWS and the third by SODEPAX.

A church of the poor

The WCC's Commission on the Church's Participation in Development made an explicit attempt at theological reflection on development following the Nairobi assembly in 1975. A forerunner was Richard Dickinson's book *To Set at Liberty the Oppressed* (1975), but the main documents are three books written or edited by Julio de Santa Ana: *Good News to the Poor* (1977), *Separation Without Hope?* (1978) and *Towards a Church of the Poor* (1979). They were followed by a document submitted to the WCC central committee in 1980 called "Towards a Church in Solidarity with the Poor". Throughout, in line with CCPD's strong convictions, this theological study was a collective effort involving many people from all around the world, and it tried to root itself in active experience.

In general this study can be heard to talk more about the church than about development. Essentially it takes the radical view that the church exists for the poor. Its concern for them is a defining characteristic — if not *the* defining characteristic — of the church's life. The church is called to preach good news to the poor. The poor must share in its life. Their concerns are to crowd into its liturgy. The church should order its priorities according to their needs, "justifying every decision by whether it helps the poor to fulfil their hopes and expectations".[1] Social responsibility is not an appendix or an optional extra but an indispensable part of the church's work. It cannot take second place to evangelism or the preaching of the word. Witness and service cannot be separated. What is said has no substance except in terms of what is done. The story of the salvation of the poor and the story of freeing them from poverty is the same story. "Churches are once again realizing that it is not possible to be the church of Jesus Christ if they fail to respond with love and justice to the challenge of the poor."[2]

All this means much more than putting the poor at the centre of attention. It involves being on their side, in solidarity with them and at one with them in their struggles. At its most intense it means that the church must be poor itself, "a church of the poor", and no longer a church without them, for "a church without the poor is a place He has obviously left".[3] The justification for such a radical vision of the church comes mainly from the Bible. God's concern for the poor is considered to be "a fundamental dimension of the biblical message".[4]

A section in the final document summarizes the evidence as follows: a vast number of biblical words relate to the problems of the poor, or to those who live in wealth at their expense; most biblical

writers from the prophets to the gospels to the epistles severely judge
the contradiction between poverty and suffering and material wealth at
the expense of suffering; a refusal to lessen the misery of the poor is
incompatible with the love of God; the year of jubilee (which was
never applied) was a call to action for distributive justice; the law or
Torah emphasizes the rights of the poor; Jesus comes to announce
good news to the poor and the year of jubilee; the salvation of the rich
depends on abandoning possessions for the benefit of the poor; Jesus
though rich himself became poor; the church itself must stand by and
share with the widow, the orphan and the dispossessed inside and
outside the Christian community; the poor are not pious because they
are poor but God is on their side; it is the rich rather than the poor who
find it hard to enter the kingdom of God; God is the God of those in
need; Jesus being poor himself was gentle and humble-hearted; to
follow him is to be like him. [5]

Historically, according to the study, instead of being closely
identified with each other, the church and the poor have grown apart.
Separation Without Hope argues that especially during the period of
Western colonial expansion and the Industrial Revolution, the poor
barely maintained a foothold within the churches. They were relegated
to the least important positions. The churches failed more than ever
before to be the champions of the poor and the poor became increasingly indifferent to the church and its gospel. A church and a gospel
for the poor did not suit the interests of the rich. Poverty, material or
spiritual, became an ideal to which some might aspire, not an offence
to God which all were required to address.

This separation, the study continues, is now being reversed most
obviously in the Third World; though even there the churches which
sprang from the missionary enterprise, converting people away from
their societies, preaching an otherworldly gospel and not always
joining in the struggle for freedom (as in India, for example), had to
win credibility. But new tendencies are now apparent, of which the
base Christian communities are a significant example.

Once we have established that the church must at least be for the
poor in a thoroughgoing way and fully involved in their struggles,
how are those struggles to be conducted? The answer reflects the
familiar and consistent approach of CCPD. Aid provided by the rich is
suspect. The New Testament church certainly shared what it had.

Those who had more shared with those who had less; though this was often the poor sharing with the poor. The rich churches of today, by contrast, have organized and institutionalized their aid or sharing so that it does not fundamentally affect their own riches. In some cases it has helped, but usually "this kind of aid has consolidated situations of domination and dependence... Poverty is not being tackled at its roots when aid is channelled in this way."[6]

If aid is not the answer, neither is the churches' participation in development, according to the study, since economic and industrial development is a process which perpetuates poverty in order that the rich can prosper. Third World systems of production have been destroyed for the benefit of First World systems. Third World countries have been reduced to suppliers of raw materials and must depend on First World capital, technology and markets if they are ever to become producers.

Structural change, not aid, is required; and it will be brought about, as we saw in the earlier debate about power, only by the poor themselves as they organize, participate and become the subjects (or take control) of their own history. "The struggle must be implemented by the poor and oppressed... *there is just no other way.*"[7] The church, if it is not itself absolutely identical with this organized struggle, must do its utmost to help it to come about and to support it. This involves not only helping the poor to organize locally to face up to immediate power structures but also to be in touch with one another on a much wider basis. Here is one of the study's proposals:

> We propose that the churches activate their various networks of support for the struggle of the poor, analyze their potential for the fight and develop means of strengthening the connectional structures that can support the struggle against poverty and oppression.[8]

If we now ask whether Christian insights have led or contributed to this conclusion, the answer, looking at the documented evidence, is "not to any great extent". Christian insights could easily be cited in its support. One of them would emphasize the more promising side of human nature. The poor like everyone else are made in the image of God and are capable of generous, courageous and imaginative achievements. It is really only natural to expect them to be full of initiatives and to take charge of their own futures. Their success will be qualified only by the odds against them. Another Christian insight would emphasize the darker side of human nature. We have a tendency, born probably of insecurity, to protect ourselves and to act in what we judge to be our own self-interest. As a result, those who happen to have power and privilege, no more or less immoral than those who have not, are most unlikely to give them up voluntarily. Both these insights point to a strategy in which the poor must and can take the initiative to bring about change, and in which all moves by the rich are suspect. Similar Christian insights could equally be cited to counsel caution. For example, if there is a darker side to human nature, it belongs to the poor just as much as to the rich.

But these and other Christian insights are not explicitly drawn upon. Instead, the option in favour of people's participation and empowering the poor to be the agents of their own liberation is said to be the result of historical and social analysis. In other words, if you study history, you see that this is in fact what happens; so to go about it in any other way is simply to fly in the face of the facts. A whole host of biblical and theological references may suggest *why* Christians become so committed to the poor, but *how* to pursue that commitment seems more a matter of "scientific analysis and interpretation of historical realities and the process of social transformation",[9] for "when we look back in history, it is clear that change has been produced by people who were not in power, but were rather looking for reform of economic, social and political structures."[10] History and social analysis, not theology, show the way — a socialist (Marxist) view of history in fact.

It could be said that these historical observations and analyses (criticized from time to time along with a Marxist analysis for claiming to be "scientific") were inaccurate, taking far too rosy a view of the achievements and abilities of the poor; and that they might have been more helpful if more room had been made for Christian insights to inform and qualify them. But the study itself offers two important reasons why we cannot be sure that the relevant and reliable Christian insights exist.

First, Christian insights are inevitably "contextual". They are coloured by the settings in which they are gained, conditioned by the people who gain them and influenced by the events in which they are involved. This will always make them partial. Someone looking from another vantage point in different circumstances will always see something else or something more. And it will almost certainly make them biased, confirming rather than undermining the view of the world that generally suits those who put them forward.

Since most readily available Christian insights, theological convictions and readings of the Bible come from Western, First World churches, which are rich much more than they are poor, they are not likely to offer the best guidance for anyone, especially the poor, seeking to decide the best strategy for overcoming poverty. The guidance offered is born of a faith and theology about sin rather than poverty, about otherworldly salvation rather than historical freedom, about being generous out of surplus wealth. It is full of abstract truths which do not relate easily to pressing problems. It is attracted to closed systems and established ways which are to be conserved rather than opened up to change. It is about a spirituality that evades the world rather than confronts it; and it is like this because it suits those with wealth and power. It springs from "the bourgeois captivity of theology". [11] It is scarcely a source of inspiration for the poor. A re-reading of biblical texts from the perspective of the poor has a very different ring about it, as an extensive account of it in *Towards a Church of the Poor* seeks to demonstrate. [12]

The second reason why relevant and reliable insights may not exist is that they cannot come out of the blue but must be gained out of the practical experience of the struggle against poverty itself. They simply cannot be had before a strategy like "people's participation" is adopted; they can be derived only from the practice of it. This insistence lies at the heart of the so-called action-reflection model of Christian obedience. Not only does this require a healthy balance of thought and activity — acting on thoughtful conclusions and thinking carefully in the light of our actions — but it also assumes that much of what we need to know will come not from our thinking but from our doing. Only in the struggle against poverty, in which God is present with the poor, shall we learn better what God is like and God's ways of changing the world for good. "The learning of the poor comes not from cool thinking remote from action, but from the struggle itself." [13]

The very theological or Christian ideas which might inform our involvement in development then need to be redefined or discovered afresh in terms of the outlook of the poor and the oppressed.

> This task cannot be carried out in comfortable study rooms and libraries. It demands a liberating practice from the theologians, from the Christian believer. It demands a commitment to struggle, a decision from the perspective of the poor and in their own terms. [14]

As a result, the study makes the following proposal:

> We propose that churches search out groups of the poor from whose struggles new theological insights may be arising, and commit resources of biblical and theological analysis to participation in those actions. We also propose that the WCC and its member churches support programmes which can help the development of theological thought rooted in the practice of the poor for justice and liberation. [15]

If then when it comes to the point of saying how Christians should be involved in the struggle against poverty, CCPD's theological contribution seems rather thin, its reply could be that the theological or Christian insights required for such a contribution are not yet to hand but must come from the poor and out of the struggle itself.

Here are at least two important points to which we must return: the "conditioned" character of our theology (that it would be different if conditions were otherwise); and the insistence that action or struggle is where we learn among other things about our faith.

Understanding diakonia

Over the last 50 years CICARWS, its predecessors and successor (Unit IV) have made several attempts to define *diakonia* or "service", one of the key words in their life. [16] In so doing they have also struggled to be clear about their own task and self-understanding. These attempts have usually been surrounded with an aura of biblical and theological reflection. Quite properly those responsible for them were concerned to root these "Christian" definitions firmly in Christian faith.

A consultation on "Contemporary Understandings of Diakonia", organized by CICARWS in Geneva in 1982, recalled three previous attempts "to define the Christian understanding of service": in Geneva in 1965, in Swanwick in 1966 and in Crete in 1978. Since 1982 two further attempts should be noted: at Larnaca in 1986 and by Unit IV in 1994. What are the sources of these understandings of *diakonia*, and how far are they derived from the Bible, theology and faith?

1. Geneva (1965)

The WCC's New Delhi assembly in 1961 had widened the understanding of inter-church aid from one of churches serving churches to one of churches serving the wider world community. Geneva 1965 broadened that understanding even further. It talked about some new directions to be followed, including above all a fresh emphasis on social action to complement more intimate and personal forms of service within families and communities:

> In a sense, the challenge of the contemporary revolution to the churches' diakonia today is to develop new policies, new concepts, new forms of action which will, on the one hand, continue to meet individual, family and wider social needs, and, on the other, promote social justice on a community, national or ecumenical world basis rather than on a strictly personal one. [17]

This emphasis on social justice was expected to meet with resistance not only because "most members of the churches today do not regard diaconal service as essential to Christian life and witness" — as it definitely is — but also because social and political action would prove to be disturbing. [18]

A second new direction for diakonia was to be sponsorship for institutional forms of service, such as homes and workshops for the disabled, in partnership with governments where desirable. Such institutions were to meet the best possible accepted standards of service. [19]

A third new direction was "to give high priority to its identification with and support for the worldwide struggles for the human rights of all men as children of God". [20]

All these proposed innovations edge towards the realm of politics.

Did these innovative, defining characteristics of diakonia grow out of an understanding of Christian faith? The consultation certainly did some work on "the theological basis of diakonia". It insisted that it is basic to the life of the church as it follows Christ's example of service;

that it depends on the presence of Christ, of which both giver and receiver may be unaware (Matthew 25); that its source is Christ's redeeming love; that deeds of service do not "justify" the church; and that service involves sacrifice.

According to the report, diakonia also aims at justice: "certainly the diakonia of the church cannot be understood in isolation from the striving for social justice". [21] The biblical basis for this claim, however, is not drawn out as it is for the others. As a result, this section on faith has little bearing on the new emphases and in particular on the widening of diakonia into social and political action, except to underline in a rather general way its importance.

The sense that these two aspects of the report — the definition of diakonia and its theological basis — are rather distant from one another is highlighted by two remarks of Leslie Cooke. First, he apologizes for the theological material. It has a long way to go. It is a fruit of 19th-century Western theology and does not yet take account of the changed situation. It is "conceived too narrowly" and does not deal with the "role of Christians to challenge the very structures of society". [22]

Later, Cooke speaks of more than one approach to the study of diakonia, including a theological approach, a "faith and order" approach, a missionary approach and his own approach, which comes "from engagement in a wide-ranging and very varied enterprise of Christian service", in other words born of practical experience. [23]

In the report the proposed redefinition of diakonia and the insights of Christian faith appear to run in parallel rather than inter-relate. What inspires the emphasis on social action is not the Bible and the faith — though well they might — but the challenges of the so-called "contemporary revolution" and "the problems of a changing dynamic society", [24] which make the more traditional intimate forms of service look inadequate left to themselves. In fact, they seem not only to challenge diakonia but also the theology of diakonia.

In this discussion of the difference that being Christian might make to aid, a curious remark by Cooke is worth noting: "These ministries of diakonia in which the churches engage are not attempts to provide a Christian counterpart to the Red Cross or an emulation on the part of the churches of... United Nations agencies..." The purpose is not only "secular-humanitarian", but to manifest Christian unity for renewal and mission. Diakonia represents "the real language needed to explain the truth of what is happening" in the churches' own "inner being". [25] In other words, it witnesses to the truth of the gospel. It begins to sound as though service is for the sake of evangelism. The advent of the International Missionary Council and growing co-operation between DICARWS and the Division on World Mission and Evangelism [26] seem to have had their effect!

2. *Swanwick 1966*

Although this week-long consultation on "Inter-Church Aid in the Next Ten Years" did not produce a summary definition of diakonia, it did arrive at three emphases highlighted by Leslie Cooke in his closing address.

First came the need (echoing Geneva the previous year) to "go beyond the organizing, the giving and the receiving of aid to a concern for changing structures". [27]

Second was the need to move beyond co-operation to community, since

> it is clear that many of the problems which face mankind can only be solved by the building of a world community, and perhaps the most significant contribution the churches can make is in manifesting that they are a world community, that they in fact share a common life in the body of Christ. [28]

Third, there was a need to move beyond the conception of service *to* the world to involvement with or service *in* the world. While "the church must always stand over against the world..., we have under-emphasized the truth that the church is in the world, that it was the world that God loved and to which he sent his only begotten son". [29]

The report of the Swanwick consultation contains many such theological and biblical allusions. It is clear about the need for "the theological undergirding of CICARWS's work". It included Bible study and a theological contribution from the Orthodox metropolitan of Calabria, Emilianos Timiadis. In it he emphasized the following points: that unless we serve we cannot be children of God; that as Christ has loved us so we must love our neighbours; that our love for our neighbour is the measure of our love for God; that we are to follow the example of Christ who came to serve and not to be served; that aid is not merely material but in solidarity, identifying with the suffering of others; that there is an intimate relationship between the sharing and offering of the eucharist and of every act of diakonia.

But if the rest of the report is anything to go by, theology was not a major feature of the consultation itself. Indeed, the report can even be heard to issue a tangential warning against too much intrusion from the "distinctive contribution of the church":

> The old ecumenical slogan "let the church be the church" is as relevant to inter-church aid as it is to faith and order or the church in society. It is the presence that ultimately matters..., a presence which is there in every situation, quietly confident in the gospel and all its promises... and therefore looking in every new situation and turn of events for some new revelation of what God has in store. [30]

Apparently following this advice itself, the consultation tended to assume the gospel and the Christian faith. Instead of drawing on them in any very deliberate way, it responded to the challenges of the situation it now faced with regard to refugees, relations with governments, the task of building new nations, the widening gap between rich and poor and the persistence of old overbearing relationships within and outside the churches. It recognized — through observation and analysis rather than theological reflection — that the poor could be served and the problems of poverty resolved only if the churches became more involved with governments in wide-ranging political and structural change.

Cooke rounded off his own major contribution to the consultation, which set out the issues to be faced, with some theological remarks. Diakonia, he said, is not merely following the example of Christ. We must conceive of what we do as "signs" (as in John's gospel), which point to Jesus as manifesting the glory of the self-giving God. He denies that to do this is "to put a theological button-hole on a paper" — an attractive but unnecessary piece of decoration. Yet the theology done at Swanwick seemed to provide an inspirational setting without really affecting the content of what the consultation had to say.

3. Crete 1978

The consultation at the Orthodox Academy in Chania, Crete, brought together CICARWS and the WCC's Orthodox Task Force to explore the Orthodox approach to diakonia. The surprisingly short report [31] is highly theological in flavour, shot through with references to the liturgy, the central performance of the church which epitomizes its faith.

Here is a summary of what was said about diakonia:

• It is a direct consequence of faith, following the example of the sacrifice (offering) of Christ, who "did not come to be served but to serve and to give up his life as a ransom for many".

• It flows from the divine liturgy, in which our offerings are sanctified by Christ.

• Like the eucharist, it is an expression of the unity of the church as the Body of Christ, offered for the material and spiritual needs of the whole world.

• It is not an optional extra but an indispensable expression of that community which has its source in the liturgy.

• It is a "liturgy after the liturgy", continuing all the themes of worship in active service. The main emphasis is not on quantity but on quality and intention, offering like the widow (Luke 21:2-3) out of the little that we have.

• It is an offering in the form of alms and collections, intended for the totality of human spiritual needs.

• It liberates humanity from poverty, oppression and penury, which are obstacles to salvation.

• It requires a simpler life-style, asceticism and sacrifice.

The report draws out three implications for the actual content of diakonia, not just affirming its importance or pointing to its motive, meaning and cost, but pointing out what has to be done: it must be holistic, meeting both emotional and spiritual needs; it must remove poverty and oppression and all that hinders salvation; and it should be macro-diakonia, on a large (some would say "structural"), even worldwide scale, tackling such issues as racism, development and ecology, because Christ's offering as a servant was for the redemption and unity of all humankind. The church must remain open and flexible regarding the form of diakonia, confronted as it is with rapid social change and a variety of complex situations.

Clearly, then, the major source of this definition or characterization of diakonia is the Christian faith as expressed in the eucharist and the divine liturgy. Here is the distinctive Orthodox contribution which has nourished and inspired ecumenical service and sharing on more than one occasion. Still, we can sense that it will turn increasingly for guidance to the dictates of what it calls "varied and adverse historical circumstances" when it comes to deciding what in practice diakonia should do.

4. Geneva 1982

This consultation on "Contemporary Understandings of Diakonia" was part of the preparation for the WCC's Vancouver assembly in 1983. Among other things, it looked for "a thorough theological discussion of diakonia which takes into account the social, economic and political contexts to which a theological understanding must speak".[32] The participants had the theological insights of Crete 1978 very much in mind and indeed rehearsed them at the outset.

Geneva 1982 produced a clear definition or characterization of diakonia in the form of eight key words. Diakonia is:

• *Essential*: Christ served and so must we. Echoing Crete, the report relates this to the eucharist, in which Christ shares with us his body.

• *Local*: institutional forms of diakonia cannot take over the responsibilities of local Christian communities.

• *Worldwide*, bringing one locality into touch with others to complement its inevitable limitations in outlook, opportunity and experience.

• *Preventative*, analyzing and dealing with the systems that deprive human beings of health and wholeness and dignity, not just easing consciences.

• *Structural* or *political*, taking action about the structural causes of human misery.

• *Humanitarian*: it is for all and potentially by all human beings. God works through individuals and groups outside the churches as well as within them.

• *Mutual*: all are givers and receivers, helped as much as helping, because all are made in God's image and have received from God and have been served by Christ.

• *Liberating*: diakonia will empower people through participation, education and accurate information about the situations that oppress and impoverish them.

The report suggests three possible sources of this definition. The first is the Christian faith and its understanding of diakonia. This was set out in Crete, as we have noted. The report adds four further points, in its section on the "Biblical and Theological Basis of Diakonia": (1) We are asked to bring good news to the poor, which includes freedom from unjust structures (Luke 4:18-19; Matthew 11:4-5). This diakonia is not optional but an essential and constitutive dimension of a lively Christian faith, for which we are accountable to our Lord (Matthew 25:31-46). (2) We look towards a new world, as the Bible promises (Isaiah 65:17-25), and are co-workers with Christ in bringing about a foretaste of it. (3) As Jesus suffered in the struggle for full human dignity and a just society, so do we (Isaiah 42 and 53). (4) Like the servant Jesus, we do not dominate, and we do not identify with the powerful (Mark 10:17-31). In addition, extensive Bible studies deal with hopes and attitudes surrounding and inspiring diakonia.

The second source of the definition appears to be contemporary needs. There is an increasing emphasis on tackling structures in response to a growing awareness of the powerful systems and organizations that relentlessly make people poor. A number of these structures are mentioned in the report itself: the economic system, transnational corporations, the debt trap, oppressive elites and development.

A third source is made quite clear in how the consultation set about its work — by organizing a series of case studies, stories about concrete expressions of Christian service from Sri Lanka, Chile, what was then the German Democratic Republic, Lebanon, South Africa and Japan. These were very practical; not one was theological in tone. They described what was actually being done; and the consultation tried to learn from this wealth of practical experience what forms diakonia should take in the future.

Overall, one is left with the impression that the relation between the theology in the report and the definition of diakonia which it puts forward is rather loose, and that where theology does make its presence felt, it says more about the reasons for serving (following Christ's example) and the style of service (humble, mutual and costly) than about the actual forms it is to take.

5. Larnaca 1986

Larnaca was the first major ecumenical consultation on inter-church aid, refugee and world service since Swanwick 1966, and it met in a very different world. The optimism of the mid-1960s about the possibilities for development had turned to a mood of frustration. The war (against poverty and oppression) was on, and, as was said more than once, that war was being lost. Some 300 people came together, among other things to "deepen their theological understanding of diakonia". The consultation theme was "Diakonia 2000 — Called to be Neighbours".

Somewhat surprisingly the Larnaca report nowhere offers even a summary definition of diakonia. Its characteristics have to be culled from the issues thrown up by small "family" groups, from the reports of the working groups organized to deal with them and from the message of the consultation, the "Larnaca Declaration".

The following points emerge from a huge amount of detail. Diakonia:

• is *comprehensive*: there are "as many kinds of diakonia as there are reactions of Christians who incarnate the love of our Lord in the situations in which they are": a better word here might have been "varied";

• is *holistic*, that is, it is part of a greater whole, along with witness and worship, from which it cannot be separated;

• is *carried out* above all *by local congregations*: the institutionalization (in hospitals and schools, for example) and professionalization of diakonia (by agencies) has made this difficult, as has the welfare state, which has taken over many of the services offered by the church;

• *focuses on people* and people's participation: once again the local congregation comes into its own; there, free from the bureaucracy which so easily excludes them, people can be energized, conscientized, equipped and organized "to have access to and a word in the determination of their fate";

• must be *global*: local communities must work together in co-responsibility for the whole inhabited earth;

• must be more *prophetic*, not repairing, but getting at root causes of injustice and the values which inspire them, replacing economic and political systems which perpetuate inequality and poverty with new ones which ensure the full participation of all people in the decisions which affect their lives;

• *protects creation* and the earth's resources;

• *involves* new forms of *sharing*, in which there is mutual giving and receiving and mutual accountability;

- cannot be separated from the struggle for *justice and peace*;
- *reaches out to all* who suffer;
- *takes its place in solidarity* with the powerless: since the powerful will not give them justice, they must therefore stand together.

Again, if we ask about the sources of this definition, at no point in the written report does it arise very explicitly out of theological reasoning — which is not to say it could not be related to the Christian faith at many points. The consultation itself included stimulating Bible studies, for example on the spiritual weapons available for warfare and the surprising and disturbing truth that our neighbour turns out to be the enemy who serves us. "Samaritan diakonia" is offered as an inspiring, biblically rooted concept, defined in terms of opting for life and faithfulness to the God of life, opposing the idolatry of the system, the self-emptying humility (*kenosis*) of the church, which learns to learn from the poor, and living in accordance with the Spirit nourished by the eucharist. None of this is incompatible with Larnaca's tacit understanding of diakonia, but very little if any of it seems to have been consciously taken into account in an effort to ensure "that our political analyses and our theological reflections nourish our diakonia and vice versa". [33]

The Latin America working group at Larnaca did offer a definition directly related to theology: "In light of our theological perspectives, we define diaconal ecclesial practice as liberating, kenotic, celebratory and hopeful." [34] But when it went on to enumerate a dozen characteristics of diakonia, many of them echoed elsewhere in the consultation, these were not related to the earlier four defining points. Similarly, the Pacific working group gave a brief definition of diakonia based on four biblical texts and then proceeded to enumerate key issues, problems and expectations and say no more about it.

Christian faith is not an explicit source of Larnaca's understanding of diakonia. Four other influences are much more obvious. One is CCPD and its emphasis on popular participation and solidarity in struggle. A second is the ongoing discussion about the ecumenical sharing of resources. Third is an explicit recognition of the frustration and fading hopes with regard to development and of much that was associated with it in favour of the struggle for justice and participation by the people. The fourth came from Larnaca's effort to practise the participation it preached, to draw on the experiences of those who came. This is why its outcome was so rich and yet so varied and hard to put into order.

Larnaca was heralded as a turning point, and its outcome was seen as a new vision of the local congregation and its gifted people as the real agents of Christian service.

6. *Johannesburg 1994*

When the WCC central committee marked the anniversary of what was now called Unit IV at its meeting in Johannesburg in 1994, yet another definition of diakonia was offered to the churches, this time by the commission of Unit IV itself. It made 11 points. Diakonia:

• puts the least advantaged first;
• is mutual, in that those who serve the needy accept their own need to receive and the ability of the needy to give;
• acts *with* those it claims to serve and not *for* them or *about* them or *over* them;
• respects the needy's own judgment as to what their needs are and how best they are met;
• adds to the power of the needy to control what happens to them;
• shares the resources that promote life;
• responds to immediate needs while understanding, resisting and transforming the systems which create and aggravate them;
• remains faithful and refuses to desert the needy — even when there are difficulties;
• acknowledges the inevitable cost as well as gain;
• gives an account of itself to those it serves;
• sets no boundaries to compassion.

No suggestion was made that these defining characteristics are derived directly from Christian faith, although it could no doubt be claimed that they are compatible with it. They were simply an attempt to gather up what the commission felt had been learned about diakonia over the years. If theological work was to be done, it lay in the future rather than the past. Diakonia was now to be practised along these lines and in so doing tested against experience and against faith. That would show best to what extent the characterization was adequate.

Looking back at this series of attempts over thirty years to define diakonia, it is fairly easy to demonstrate that the explicit relationship between them and Christian insights is rather weak. Christian insights are not often seen to be contributing to the substance of diakonia, illuminating and informing what it should actually be doing. Historical pressures and practical experience seem to be more influential. We are left again with a number of questions to pick up later. What do we make of these "non-theological" influences? If the influence of faith is not explicit, does that mean it is non-existent? Is faith's contribution to be sought and expected equally at every point? Is it sufficient to see whether our ideas about diakonia are compatible with faith once we have developed them, rather than let faith take the lead?

The search for theology

When the joint WCC-Roman Catholic Committee on Society, Development and Peace (SODEPAX) went "In Search of a Theology of Development" at a consultation in Cartigny, Switzerland, in 1969, it seems to have discovered many theologies: prophetic, pastoral, systematic, ethical, spiritual and ecumenical, not to mention a preliminary outline by Gustavo Gutiérrez of what would later become known as a "theology of liberation". But if we ask about relating theology or Christian faith to development, there seem to be, broadly speaking, only two ways.

The first is to take a Christian insight, teaching or doctrine and draw out its implications for development and the struggle against poverty. John Bennett, for example, took "the Christian understanding of man" as a union of the spiritual and material, concluding that a person cannot develop as a spiritual being if material requirements are neglected. Again he talked about the "essential goodness" of creation, which should lead us to encourage rather than stifle inventiveness (in science and technology) as humanity seeks to rid the world of poverty. David Jenkins pointed out that, according to Jesus, the (powerful) way God works and achieves the kingdom is through powerlessness. This should lead us to question the effectiveness of playing the power game and to recognize that powerlessness, in the form of suffering, absorption, reconciliation and love, is "the one constantly creative and open-ended force at work in the world". Christian teaching thus has strategic implications. Jürgen Moltmann, discussing Christian hope, concluded that we should put more emphasis on our imagined desires and longings than on the future we can calculate and forecast from

what we — or rather the powerful — are presently able to do; and that
if we want to make a start on achieving that future, we should go with
the Crucified, not with those who "represent the advanced achievements of society, but with their victims". [35]

It was freely acknowledged that when we try to draw out Christian
insights in this way, not all of them will prove to be equally relevant or
illuminating.

The second way of relating faith and development starts with the
questions that arise when we get involved in practical actions and then
see what faith has to say about them and whether it can help to resolve
them. This was one reason why the consultation came about at all —
in response to important questions which had been thrown up by the
Church and Society conference in Geneva in 1966 and the Uppsala
assembly of 1968, not least about "revolution". Other questions raised
at the consultation included how we properly motivate people to
change, what we make of the effects of development on the social
structures of underdeveloped countries, the role of the church in
politics, what we are to make of urbanization and the modern secular
city, the benefits and drawbacks of growing abundance. The questions, large and small — some of them dated, others still relevant
25 years later — are numerous and varied, and found on almost every
page of the report.

But having discovered the questions, how does one proceed with
them? How are useful connections to be made between these concrete
issues and Christian insights and theological thinking? If the aim of
the consultation was to establish some kind of methodology, it had to
acknowledge its failure. [36] Nevertheless, a number of useful points
were made.

First, regardless of how helpful theology may turn out to be, it
cannot answer the questions by itself. Other disciplines like economics need to be involved. Theology may contribute some useful
insights but it cannot contribute all the insights that are required.

Second, there is a danger of considering only those areas of
Christian teaching that promise to be relevant and helpful and acceptable, instead of looking at faith in the round. Issues should be dealt
with "as much as possible in the total context of the Christian faith". [37]

Third, we must be clear about whether the questions raised by
the struggle and those raised by the Christian faith, to which we turn

for some kind of response, are talking about the same things. Are the history of our salvation (as it might be called) and the history of our struggle for a better life in this world two different histories or one and the same reality? Gutiérrez, who discusses this issue at length, is emphatic that they are the same — "to work to transform this world is in itself salvation"[38] — but his conclusion is obviously debatable.

Fourth, both the questions that are asked and what are claimed to be the Christian insights about faith, hope, human nature, power, wealth or whatever, will be coloured by the experience and outlook and circumstances of those who put them forward. They are inevitably biased and we have to find ways of taking this bias into account. When, for example, Philip Land poses nine questions or problems of development "which need the further attention of theologians", it is obvious with hindsight that the questions came from someone well-disposed towards modernization and the then-current theology of the "Secular City", which tended to sanctify it.[39]

Fifth, instead of relating questions to particular Christian insights rather narrowly, it may be better to relate them to the main sources of rather varied insights, such as the biblical teaching on a certain theme or the historical treatment of a doctrine like creation or the Christian ethical tradition regarding topics like revolt and civil disobedience. The emphasis is on a wealth of insights to be considered rather than on a single defined truth with which the question has to come to terms.

These two ways of relating faith and development, one by drawing out the implications of Christian insights, the other (which predominates in the report) by starting with the questions and seeing what faith has to say in reply, are by no means discrete or mutually exclusive. They are in fact compatible and complementary. Those who follow the first way do not spell out the implications of their faith in a vacuum; invariably, they already have a problem or question in mind. John Bennett did when he explored the Christian understanding of human nature: he was wondering about the extent to which economic development and material progress are legitimate aspects of making the world more human. David Jenkins had a question in mind when he explored the seeming powerlessness of Christ: he was wondering how we can actually move the world on to become more human. The question may be unstated, and a rather narrow range of

Christian teaching may be brought to bear on it, but a question is there all the same.

Similarly, when we adopt the second approach and look to see what the various traditions of faith might have to say about our questions, the time will come when we have to make up our minds what we do think faith is saying, particularly what it is saying to us, and then move on to draw out the implications for our own future practice.

In other words, these two approaches are better understood as two phases in a single cycle or continuous exchange which raises issues of development (or any other aspect of practical obedience), looks for relevant commentaries on them within the Christian tradition, decides what insights and advice are being offered and then works out the implications of behaving as if those insights were true.

Three other kinds of theological activity are referred to in the SODEPAX search: defining concepts, social ethics and discerning what God is doing.

First, work is done to arrive at certain guiding concepts and make them satisfactory. Often these are referred to as "theologies" of this or that or the other. More accurately, they should be called "theories", since theologies, strictly speaking, talk about God. CICARWS, as we have seen, made repeated attempts to define the concept of diakonia. SODEPAX most obviously worked at a concept (or "theology" or "theory") of development. It debated various options. Technology and modernization no longer commanded the respect they once did. A rising standard of living and material progress are good but insufficient. Development as presently understood seemed to bring benefits to some at an unacceptable cost to others. Liberation from all that oppresses and frustrates human hopes and aspirations seemed more appropriate and promising, but incomplete. If liberation is freedom *from* there must also be a responsible and creative freedom *for*.

The search for and use of these concepts or theories can be seen as part of the same cycle we have already described, which relates faith to development and development to faith. Obviously, this search is responding to very basic questions thrown up in the course of practical obedience: What are the effects of what we are doing? What should we be about (especially if what we are about now is proving to be unsatisfactory)? What should we be trying to achieve? In an attempt to deal with them all sorts of insights are brought into play including economic, political, social as well as Christian. One discipline on its own will not do. The result is an "answer" in rather general and abstract terms. It is more complex than a single Christian insight to which we then seek to be true in practice, such as our understanding of human beings as both material and spiritual by nature. It may have drawn on many Christian insights as well as those from different disciplines. It has however endeavoured to take Christian insights into account. It could therefore be described as "Christian" teaching. It is not purely derived from Christian faith, but it is certainly informed by Christian faith. To complete the cycle, we then come to the point where, if we say this is the kind of thing (liberation, for example) that we ought to be about when we are involved in development, we have to live and act as if it were true, or draw out its implications in practice. So these "concepts", complex as they are, become insights which guide and shape what we are doing.

Second, SODEPAX refers, though only in passing, to Christian social ethics as part of what is meant by the "theology of development". [40] Without discussing at length the distinction between theology and ethics, [41] we should note that some of the questions thrown up by our involvement with development are "*ought* questions", asking what we ought to do and how we ought to go about it, and others are "*is* questions", asking what is going on here, what is most likely to achieve results and what are the possibilities. Both require careful empirical research; but when it comes to relating them to Christian faith, the former are dealt with by Christian ethics and Christian social ethics, the latter by theology. The cycle is much the same in each case: we start with the question or problem; we see what either the ethical or theological teachings of Christianity have to say about it; we draw on other disciplines; and then we try to draw out the implications, asking what it would mean to live as if this were right (ethics) or true (theology).

The connection between ethics and theology is that ethics finally depends on theology. What *ought* to be depends on what we believe *is* the case. For example, because we believe that human beings *are* both material and spiritual by nature, both their material and spiritual needs *ought* to be met; because they *are* made as created beings in the image of God, they *ought* to be free to exercise their creativity.

Third, SODEPAX talks of the theology that discerns what God is doing or God's actions in events. [42] Sometimes (though not consistently) this is referred to as "prophetic theology". [43] Here and elsewhere, to say that God is doing something almost always amounts to pointing out what we approve of and what we don't. It is a rather dressed-up way of referring to the judgments we eventually have to make when we answer the questions raised by our attempts at obedience. It can be a rather dangerous way of confusing God's opinions and enthusiasms with our own.

Overall, then, we might suggest that a better name for the SODEPAX consultation than "In Search of a Theology of Development" would have been "In Search of a Way of Relating Theology and Development". The report admits that the search was not completed, and it would be interesting to speculate how much further it has progressed since then. But the consultation did throw up a number of clues: the need to take other disciplines into account, not being over-selective about which Christian teachings we consider, being confident that our faith is talking about our world and not some other and recognizing that all our questions and insights are inevitably biased.

Answering the question

In the light of these three case studies we must now return to the original question about the difference that being "Christian" makes to aid. In fact, this breaks down into several different questions: Has being "Christian" made a difference? Should it make a difference — and if so how? And if it should but has failed, what might be the reasons for the failure?

It is not difficult to conclude on the basis of the written evidence that Christian faith has served as little more than a gloss, or "a theological button-hole on a paper", or a rather superficial piece of window dressing. Christians may be quite eloquent when they talk about the absolute necessity to struggle alongside the poor or about the motives for doing so, such as following the example of Christ and responding to the kindness of God. There is confident talk about the broad characteristics or style of our involvement, the likely cost of our endeavours and the hope we have of succeeding. But all of this seems to be on the edges of what the questioner had in mind when referring to "Oxfam with hymns". She was asking about what we actually do rather than all the fine reasons for doing it or the hopes that surround it. And here, according to the evidence, the Christian faith seems to have had much less to say, and has not made too much of a difference. It has not been entirely silent, but other voices, such as common sense born of experience and the harsh realities and challenges of the contemporary world, which are there for all to see, Christian or not, seem to be far more vocal and influential.

Such a negative conclusion however requires at least one immediate and massive qualification. Our discussion has tended to assume that Christian faith can guide and shape what we do in development and elsewhere only by speaking out in direct and obvious ways. But it may be far more influential at a less self-conscious level by forming Christians to be certain kinds of people who then think and behave, almost without knowing what they do, as the people they have become. Immersed in the Christian tradition and in the Christian community and above all in the liturgy, they grow into the mind of Christ, and it is that "mind" rather than a great deal of conscious reasoning which makes all the difference. If they cannot always be sharply differentiated in their views and commitments from others who do not name the name of Christ, it may be because those others are also baptized and formed to some extent by the same Christian culture, whose effects come not only as a result of conscious choice. Many humanitarian organizations, including Oxfam, are examples of this.

The extent to which Christian faith ought to make a difference in the areas the questioner had in mind, whether we are organizing for political protest or setting up and running a programme of community development, is not so clear. When it comes to our motives for doing these things, our good hopes, the cost we are prepared to shoulder, our perseverance, humility and love, there is not much doubt. Again, it is not difficult to see how Christian insights can contribute to general concepts like "development" and "diakonia". But when it comes to what we actually decide to do or to support, we need to remind ourselves again of the need to turn to other disciplines like economics, politics, development studies, agronomy and medicine. They can severely qualify the directions that faith might otherwise take. They can challenge and inform its inclinations and judgments. They can be as influential and, in some cases, even more so. The qualified agriculturalist without faith will be preferable to an ignorant believer full of good intentions but bad advice. The Christian as Christian will find it hard to choose between one economist's technique for achieving a specified result and another's.

It is generally agreed that these other disciplines, which may be decisive, can be pursued in their own right by Christians and non-Christians. At this level we may feel that they have more to contribute than Christian faith, and we may be relieved rather than worried when the conclusions reached are much the same for Christians and non-Christians. But we should remember that what are sometimes referred to as "autonomous" disciplines (recognized as working to their own rules) and "experts" have their own motives and hopes which influence what they do. While their expertise should be respected, their motives, goals and values — why they do what they do and to what end — are still open to question. They are not immune to the challenges of Christian faith. [44]

On the evidence we have been looking at, one obvious reason why we fail to bring Christian faith to bear on practice is that when we come to the point where hard thinking needs to be done, we remain uncertain as to how to set about it. Talk about "action-reflection" models has even been heard to cast doubt on the need for much hard thinking at all!

We must neither overestimate nor underestimate the place for hard thinking, which presumably involves carefully gathering and weighing the evidence, following through the logic of the argument, taking a variety of considerations into account, facing up to contradictions, ironing out inconsistencies, coming to solidly based conclusions and so on. We overestimate the place for it if we forget three things. The first is that Christian obedience and discipleship is more than getting our intellectual ideas into order (abstract Western theology has sometimes given the impression that this is really all that matters, so that theology can go on breeding theology in its own self-contained world). Christian discipleship is getting our actions right; and our thinking in the end is the servant of what we do. Reflection must always be the good companion of action in the pastoral cycle of action and reflection.

The second point to remember is that we learn and gain insights from our involvement in action just as much as — if not more than —

we do by trying to think things through. This is partly why CCPD has placed such emphasis on people's movements and people's participation and why practical experience has been a constant source of insight for CICARWS. The point is taken too far if it insists that we learn *only* by doing, that disciplined attempts to sort out what we think and gather up what we have learned — in other words, to develop expertise — are of little importance.[45]

Third, we should not forget that unsystematic ways of reflecting can be highly productive. The practice of the base Christian communities is the best-known example of this. Questions thrown up by their day-to-day struggles are juxtaposed with passages from the Bible. I well remember an impassioned reading of the story of Naboth's vineyard (1 Kings 21) by landless people in Brazil. Sparks fly, connections are made, insights are gained, but without a great deal of formality or logic or carefully constructed procedures.[46]

While the place for hard and careful thinking should be kept in perspective, the need for it remains; but when it finally comes to it, the evidence suggests we have been at something of a loss as to how to proceed. SODEPAX admitted this in 1972, and it is not clear that much progress has been made subsequently, despite a good deal of writing about "doing theology". How to do it is often referred to as a question of "methodology".

Ecumenical Christian social ethics, represented in the WCC over the last 50 years by Church and Society and by notable conferences such as Geneva 1966, seems to have been more confident in this respect and more productive. It seems to have moved with more assurance between the insights of faith, broad principles and practical details. It seems to have known how to take other disciplines into account and where to be cautious about making direct links between faith and practice. It developed concepts like the Responsible Society, which offered goals and criteria for moving towards them. It addressed itself to many of the economic and political issues relevant to the work of Inter-Church Aid and Refugee and World Service, not least when the latter became increasingly concerned with politics and power. There was certainly contact between them, even if it does not appear to have been as persistent or mutually supportive as it might have been.

If Church and Society did not lose confidence in itself, it seems in time to have lost the confidence of others. It was criticized for being elitist (with its emphasis on "experts" and "study") and out of sympathy with people's participation and with action and reflection as ways of charting the course of Christian obedience. It was also thought by some to be too Western and too conservative in its "responsible" approach to society, and out of sympathy with the more radical and revolutionary stirrings coming from the Third World. Justified or not, this loss of confidence meant that the carefully developed approaches of Church and Society came to mark differences of opinion rather than a growing consensus about "methodology".

Relating faith and practice

A method of relating Christian faith and its insights to the practice of development or to the struggle against poverty and for life can either be fairly simple or very complicated. If it is to have any chance of being followed, it should be simple, but without entirely forgetting that it is probably very complicated. The following four points are aimed at simplicity even if the first one at least is contentious.

1. We need to be more confident that it is at least worth trying to relate Christian faith to development: that faith is relevant, that it really is, as Gutiérrez put it, talking about our world and our history and not some other.

Christian insights are not foreign bodies floating down from another world and having little if anything of interest to say about this one. Like all other insights, they are the result of reflecting on what we experience, testing our conclusions against further experience and distilling them into "truths" and "principles", "teachings" and "doctrines" and "rules". The only experiences we have to reflect on are those we encounter for ourselves or hear about from others. They may be extraordinary experiences that tend to colour everything else, like an exodus from Egypt, or the living and dying of Jesus of Nazareth, or the fall of Rome, or Auschwitz. They are part of everything else all the same. The biblical writers, for example, talk about their experiences in this world, in the cities and villages, families and communities in which they lived, in peace and war, famine and plenty, under good rulers and bad. The doctrines and teachings of the church are the fruit of long reflection by the members of the church on their experiences in the same world. Christian ethical codes are the result of experiencing in this world, usually over a lengthy period of time, what seems to work for good and what does not. Thus when we put questions about this world to them, they at least know what we are talking about. They are on the same ground as we are and they have observations to make about it. We can go to them in the confidence that if we listen and dig around we shall find useful material.

2. Our confidence can be further increased when we recognize another similarity between the questions we ask and the insights which Christian faith — and other disciplines like economics and agriculture — have to offer us. All are bewildering in their variety, but all share the same three major concerns: (1) to *analyze* or understand the world and the people we are dealing with, (2) to *set goals* for our endeavours to change things for good and solve our problems, and (3) to *find ways* and means of achieving what we set out to do.

In development as elsewhere, we want to know what we are dealing with (a benign process which will finally benefit everyone, a demonic one which only entrenches poverty and injustice or something in between?), because if we get our analysis wrong we cannot hope to make an appropriate response. We want to know where we ought to be going and what we are out to achieve (economic growth, for example, or sharing and taking care of what we already have or something far more comprehensive?), because we need a sense of direction. We want to know how to get from where we are to where we want to be (by modernization, for example, or by participation or revolution or reform?) or at least how to take the next step. Almost any discipline we might mention — from politics to economics to medicine to agriculture — addresses those same three concerns. And so does Christian faith.

For example, when faith talks about the nature of women and men, sin or the powers of this dark world, it is talking about "what we are dealing with". When it talks about the kingdom, the new earth, the nature of a Christian community or freedom, it is talking about "what we are out to achieve". When it talks about the work of salvation and redemption, it is talking about "how to get from where we are to where we want to be".

A less abstract example comes from the experience of the base Christian communities immersed in the struggles of the poor. As we have said, almost any story or passage from the Bible is the outcome of reflection by the writers and the communities they belong to on their experiences in this world, however extraordinary those experiences may be. How are they to understand the nature of riches, for example, or the ebb and flow of powers and empires in the ancient world? What should they hope to make of it all and where and how do they begin? There is nothing else but these mundane realities for them to reflect on. So when we bring our questions to these passages, questions thrown up by our daily life about poverty and power among other things, we will find, if we dig, that they too have things to say about the "what", the "where" and the "how".

There is therefore an underlying simplicity about putting the questions we ask alongside the insights of Christian faith and of other disciplines and allowing them to inform each other. They are all dealing with the same world and with the same basic concerns as to what that world is like and should be like and how it could be changed.

3. But no matter how exhaustively we put our questions, none of this highly relevant material, including the Bible and the teachings of Christianity, will automatically produce the answers for us. We are simply gathering more material to work on. We are ensuring that the answers, which must be our own, do not come out of unnecessarily empty heads. The different disciplines will immensely nourish our thinking, but they will not think for us, unless we choose to give to any of them authority over us — out of respect or fear or laziness or conformity or weariness. At the end of the day, drawing on whatever insights are available and thinking as rigorously as we know how, we have to make of them what we can for ourselves. We must finally supply the answers to the questions we raise and then practise the mature obedience which is true to them. No method, however carefully or elaborately worked out, will do that for us.

4. Finally, we should not exaggerate the tension between the two methods of relating Christian faith and insights to aid and development and our Christian practice in general, so that we consider them to be diametrically opposed to each other. Echoes of such a polarization are often heard. Here are four examples. The first contrasts the abstract and the concrete; the second, truth derived from doctrine and

from particular situations; the third, daily struggle and doctrinal debate; the fourth, problem-solving and Christian testimony.

> It is rather easy to make an idealistic and abstract appraisal of Christian service... But our task is to engage in positive participation and concrete involvement in search of the forms of Christian service in the contemporary world which meet real and deep needs. [47]

> [At one time] we would have perhaps tried to establish what the Christian doctrines and teachings were on the subject, and to deduce certain consequences in order to draw up a programme. We have in a way reversed the order..., trying to understand the struggle of the poor, then reflect theologically to decide the strategy... In the Western tradition, [theology] is a process aimed at determining, explicating and possibly vindicating the correct doctrine... in order to derive from it correct Christian action... In the Scriptures we find very few instances, if any, of such a process of theologizing... What we usually find there is the story of a particular situation of the people of God, and how the word of God comes to comfort, to admonish, to command, to advise, to correct or to condemn... [48]

> The theological diversity among the units and sub-units of the Council is perceived by some as a sign of vitality, by others as a sign of too little integration and too much division. For some, there is still too great a distance between the daily struggles and anguish of human life and the technical, theological discussions of traditional doctrinal questions. [49]

> The witness of the church at the end of this violent century should be, not a list of problems and solutions, but "a statement of facts and meaning in indissoluble unity", proceeding from the churches' testimony itself. [50]

The two methods can easily be characterized, not to say caricatured. One method allows the world with its pressing questions and insights gained from experience, together with the pervasive outlooks of the day (whether socialist or Marxist or liberal or capitalist) to take the lead. The other looks to the more abstract or given generalities of faith to take the initiative, challenging, enriching, surprising and shaping the world with what it has to say.

Such inevitable tensions and different emphases are not fundamentally incompatible or necessarily opposed to one another. They belong to the same cycles of question and response, action and reflection, experiencing, learning and implementing. The Christian faith is both the child and the guardian of experience. Experience is both the midwife and the pupil of Christian faith.

To summarize, when the "pastoral cycle" of reflecting on action and acting in the light of reflection comes to the stage of hard thinking, it will first remember the three questions it has to tackle: what are we dealing with? what do we want to achieve? and how do we achieve it? Second, it will search the relevant disciplines, including the Bible and Christian teaching, and collect their replies to those three questions. Third, having absorbed them as best it can and noting where they complement each other, agree or disagree, it will draw its own conclusions and go on to act in ways that are true to them.

We have so far omitted one crucial factor referred to in the three case studies on CCPD, Diakonia and SODEPAX. Everything involved in relating Christian faith to development is highly conditioned, or contextual, or relative, or biased: the questions we ask, the insights offered by various disciplines, the teachings of Christian faith, the selection of what we take notice of and what we pass over, the decisions about what to do next. Above all the people who ask the questions and produce the insights out of their reflections on experience — and who eventually have to make up their minds and take the decisions — are conditioned. If the conditions or circumstances had been different, as they are for other people at other times and in other places, then the questions and the insights and decisions would have been different.

All that we wonder about and think and do is inevitably affected by the kinds of people we are, our temperaments, our histories, our surroundings, our limited horizons, our interests, fears, needs and perversities. Sometimes these conditions are so pervasive that we even mistake them for Christianity itself. When that happens, Christian aid is no different from everybody else's aid because it has completely adopted the outlook and assumptions and value systems that condition everybody else. These continuing factors cannot be avoided. We cannot rise above them to gain absolute or universal truths, but we can acknowledge them and compensate for them as best we can.

We do so by fostering a certain modesty and self-awareness. We acknowledge that we are limited human beings who are always to some extent going to be wrong. But we compensate for this chiefly by opening ourselves up to as wide and varied a "community of dis-agreement" as we can find. It will be full of people as limited and conditioned and mistaken as we are, but fortunately they will be limited and conditioned and mistaken in different ways. If we open up to them, there is some hope that their insights, whatever their shortcomings and idiosyncrasies, will challenge and complement and correct ours and ours theirs, so that together the questions we ask and the insights we bring to bear and the conclusions we reach will be more adequate than had we been left to ourselves.

That is one important reason why, in the struggle against poverty and the endeavour to make it a Christian struggle, the rich and powerful must learn from the poor and the powerless, as CCPD for example has so often insisted. The theology and experience of the prosperous is not universal. It is highly conditioned by their prosperity. But neither rich nor poor must fall into the romantic error of thinking that the voice of the poor (or of the "people"), for all its importance, is less partial and limited in its perspectives than all other voices. A theology of liberation, for example, is not universal any more than is Western theology. To put the poor first as God's priority is never to put them above question.

Church aid and ecumenical aid

The particular struggle against poverty and for life which we have been reviewing and discussing gains its identity not only by being Christian but also by being of the churches and by being ecumenical.

There is no doubt that it is intrinsic to the mission of the church to be on the side of the poor and to respond to human need, or that such a response ought to be shaped by the church's faith, even if the result is not always different from everybody else's response. But none of this quite answers the question as to whether there is any need for separate church organizations to carry out this response.

Many have answered this question affirmatively and have founded, among other things, Christian hospitals and Christian agencies for relief, aid and development. Some have answered negatively, preferring to leave the responsibility with the churches as such and their local congregations, or to support individual Christians as they go out from the churches and take their place in secular institutions and agencies.

It would be foolish to look for a single answer to a question that has to be tackled in a variety of cultural and historical contexts. Even within Europe the appropriateness of "church" institutions, whether hospitals, agencies, parties or schools, varies from one country to another.

Apart from such variables several other considerations need to be borne in mind. First, our Christian faith may lead us at times to such a distinctive approach to poverty that the church has to go it alone. No one else will cooperate and no one else will do it or can do it in quite this way if the church does not. Second, a separate church agency may be called for in order to mobilize the churches either separately or ecumenically and offer them the challenge, encouragement, expertise and co-ordination they need if they are to rise to their calling. Third, actions and agencies labelled "church" may be required in order to make the church's response visible to the wider world, not merely as a matter of self-promotion but as a matter of witness.

Fourth, and this may be a way of summarizing the other three, there may be very real advantages in creating church institutions which enable the churches to maximize their potential for effective action. The balance sheet should at least be drawn up. They may of course be misunderstood as having narrow sympathies, but internationally, for example, the churches represent the most extensive and impressive transnational "corporation" in the world. In all its variety, the church still has a strong corporate identity and sense of mission. The churches may yet need to seize the advantages that an international church agency could bring, not to private investors by moving capital around the world, but to the poorest of the poor by deploying its considerable resources at international, regional, national and local levels.

The word "ecumenical" has come to have several meanings within the circles of inter-church aid as elsewhere.

First and historically, the ecumenical movement has had to do with the unity and renewal of the churches. By being drawn together and into unity they are to be renewed, and by being renewed they will be drawn together. But there has been a running debate as to how far the struggle with the poor unites the churches or divides them even further. In early days it was often said that "doctrine divides and service unites". Later the growing influence of the churches of the

Third World and of the poor led to confrontation. More recently, the question has been raised again as to whether the issues of "life and work" (in contrast to "faith and order"), however divisive they can be, are not the real ground on which unity must be built. Wherever the truth lies, the struggle with the poor for life can never be for the sake of promoting the unity of the churches.

Second, "ecumenical" has been used to identify the family or tribe to which we belong and to insist that family membership carries with it responsibilities. Our first loyalties lie with the family. Everything possible should be done to work with it and to build it up. Disputes within it should be settled and not used as reasons for turning elsewhere. There is a family way of behaving. Ecumenical disciplines, such as the guidelines for ecumenical resource sharing, should be observed.

Third, "ecumenical" refers not to one church but to one world and to the unity of the members of all faiths for the sake of the whole inhabited earth. Unity negotiations between churches are at best secondary to those between the different peoples, rich and poor, variously coloured, of all the world. Common ground between Christians, as important as that may be, takes second place to finding common ground between peoples of all faiths and of none. The lesser unity or ecumenism welcomes and seeks to serve the greater. Such an understanding casts a different, less defensive light on our attitude to the question about "Oxfam with hymns". At times we may regret that a necessary difference required by faith is not apparent. And we should always regret it when we have neglected to allow our faith to nourish and inspire our involvement in aid and development, whatever the upshot may be and whether or not there is any great difference at the end of the day. But when there is very little difference between us, we may sometimes want to rejoice. We have found good things in common and this is not the denial but the fulfilment of our ecumenism.

Finally, we return to the conditional or relative nature of all our questions and answers, insights and actions in relation to poverty. "Ecumenical" can be used to name a community (of all Christians or even more inclusive) which is worldwide, immensely diverse and marked by inevitable disagreement. Whatever other reasons there may be for living in such a community and so being "ecumenical", it is required by a proper understanding of the nature of Christian reflection on action, since only openness to an ecumenical community, difficult as it is to achieve in practice, can offer the criticism, correction, comprehensiveness and complementarity which is required if we are to have any hope of seeing and doing the truth.

NOTES

[1] J. de Santa Ana, ed., *Towards a Church of the Poor*, Geneva, WCC, 1979, p.196.
[2] *Towards a Church in Solidarity with the Poor*, Geneva, WCC, 1980, p.17.
[3] J. de Santa Ana, *op. cit.*, p.15.
[4] *Ibid.*, p.x.
[5] See *Towards a Church in Solidarity with the Poor* pp.18-20.
[6] J. de Santa Ana, *op. cit.*, pp.184f.
[7] *Ibid.*, p.76; italics in original.
[8] *Ibid.*, p.202.
[9] *Ibid.*, p.xxii.
[10] *Ibid.*, pp.162f.
[11] *Ibid.*, p.117.
[12] See *ibid.*, pp.139-55.
[13] *Ibid.*. p.198.
[14] *Ibid.*, p.72.
[15] *Towards a Church in Solidarity with the Poor*, p.25; see *Towards a Church of the Poor*, p.198.
[16] For a survey, see M. Robra, "Theological and Biblical Reflection on Diakonia", in *The Ecumenical Review*, Vol. 46, no. 3, Geneva, WCC, 1994, p.276.
[17] *The Role of the Diakonia of the Church in Contemporary Society*, Geneva, WCC, 1966, p.34.
[18] *Ibid.*, p.47.
[19] See *ibid.*, p.50.
[20] *Ibid.*, p.34.
[21] *Ibid.*, p.18.
[22] *Ibid.*, p.8.
[23] *Ibid.*, p.57.
[24] *Ibid.*, p.48.
[25] *Ibid.*, pp.60f.
[26] *Ibid.*, p.59.
[27] *Digest of the 1966 world consultation on Inter-Church Aid*, Geneva, WCC, 1966, pp.126f.
[28] *Ibid.*, pp.129f.
[29] *Ibid.*, p.130.
[30] *Ibid.*, pp.131f.
[31] *The Orthodox Approach to Diakonia*, Geneva, WCC, 1980.
[32] *Contemporary Understandings of Diakonia*, Geneva, WCC, 1983, p.15.

136   *Not Angels but Agencies*

33 K. Poser, ed., *Called to be Neighbours*, Geneva, WCC, 1987, p.88.

34 *Ibid.*, p.113.

35 *In Search of a Theology of Development*, Geneva, SODEPAX, 1969, p.96.

36 See *ibid.*, p.33.

37 *Ibid.*, p.72.

38 *Ibid.*, p.146.

39 See *ibid.*, pp.180-203.

40 *Ibid.*, p.32; cf. R.H. Preston, *Confusions in Christian Social Ethics*, London, SCM, 1994; I. Linden, *Back to Basics*, London, CIIR, 1994.

41 See M. Taylor, *Good for the Poor*, London, Mowbray, 1990, ch. 1.

42 *In Search of a Theology of Development*, pp.18, 37.

43 *Ibid.*, pp.18, 40.

44 On this point, see A. Padilha, in *The Ecumenical Review*, Vol. 46, no. 3, 1994, p.287.

45 On this see R.H. Preston, *op.cit.*

46 See E. Cardenal, *The Gospel in Solentiname*, Maryknoll NY, Orbis, 1976; W.S. Robins, ed., *Through the Eyes of a Woman*, Geneva, WCC/YWCA, 1995.

47 W.A. Visser 't Hooft, ed., *New Delhi Report*, Geneva, WCC, 1962, p.111 .

48 J. Míguez Bonino, "The Struggle of the Poor and the Church", *The Ecumenical Review*, Vol. 27, no. 1, 1975, pp.36-38.

49 D. Gill, ed., *Gathered for Life*, Geneva, WCC, 1983, pp.249.

50 C.L. Patijn, "The Responsible Society in Retrospect", *The Ecumenical Review*, Vol. 40, 1988, p.370. The quotation is from Lesslie Newbigin, *The Other Side of 1984*.

6. An Agenda for Jubilee

So what of the future? In 1992 four agencies (Bread for the World and EZE in Germany, ICCO in the Netherlands and Christian Aid), faced with the persistence of poverty and growing numbers of poor people in the world, agreed to look together at the whole range of their work to see where it could be improved and whether they could discern a way forward. They decided to carry out the review themselves, using their own staff to gather evidence from North and South. But they also asked the WCC's Commission on the Churches' Participation in Development (CCPD) to bring together a group of experienced people from the South to review matters from their very different perspective. Representatives of all three main groups of the ecumenical family, as we have defined it, were therefore involved: agencies, national councils of churches and the WCC itself.

Four documents were produced: one by the South, one by the North, one by a meeting of both North and South in Berlin in September 1993, and one by the directors of the four agencies. [1]

The conclusions of "Discerning the Way Together" on such issues as poverty in the North, gender, education, health, agriculture and population do not amount to a single, unified vision of the future, its goals or strategies. This is partly because all involved were wary of global answers, believing that the way forward would differ from place to place. But many of the conclusions do show continuity with our own review of the ecumenical response to poverty over the last fifty years and do address the unfinished agenda of the wider ecumenical family. The same can be said of a special issue of *The Ecumenical Review* called "Ecumenical Diakonia: New Challenges, New Responses", published in July 1994 to "mark the fiftieth anniversary of sharing and service within the worldwide ecumenical movement".

We shall refer to it in this chapter as "Ecumenical Diakonia". Three obvious examples of following up the unfinished agenda have to do with partnership, empowerment and theology.

Partnership

The ideals and rhetoric of partnership are rehearsed in the "Discerning the Way Together" documents as they were in the ecumenical family's previous attempts to define diakonia, in the Guidelines for Sharing drawn up at El Escorial and in its talk of "ecumenical discipline". Partnership is still characterized by equality between those who share a common faith and common objectives, by mutual trust, by giving and receiving and by accountability to each other. Relationships between partners will be open (or "transparent"). There are to be no secrets. Decisions will be shared. An underlying or special family commitment will bind the partners together and prove stronger in the long term than failures and disappointments along the way.

But if the ideals are still there, so is the recognition of repeated failure to achieve them. Old "colonial" attitudes have re-emerged — if they ever went away. The mistakes of the missionary movements are repeated. Agency staff can be overbearing. The South is not really party to decisions. Shared decision-making is said to be difficult in practice. The presence of agency offices and expatriate staff in Southern countries spells for many the very opposite of trust. North and South do not always share the same faith or priorities, or even know each other all that well. The North regards the South as inefficient. The fact that the word "partner" is used far more often by the North of the South than by the South of the North reveals unequal rather than equal relationships.

With the recognition of failure comes the acknowledgment that there is little point in simply exhorting the guilty parties to do better. A more realistic response is required, and both "Discerning the Way Together" and "Ecumenical Diakonia" have suggestions to make. [2]

One possibility is to accept that the funding agencies of the North simply cannot sustain the sort of relationships being described, and certainly not so many of them as they have pretended to do in the past. Many in future will have to be far more superficial and more like business contracts with clients. Agencies will then be free to develop a few relationships at a deeper level. This will involve ending some partnerships and withdrawing from some countries. The implication is that, given time and opportunity, partnership can succeed. It is probably a false hope.

Another possibility is reflected in recent discussions about national councils of churches. What they have been offered is "capacity building", which is something less than partnership. It largely amounts to training to manage their staff and programmes and to account for the money they spend in ways more acceptable and reassuring to Northern agencies and governments, who are insisting more and more on knowing that "their" money is being well spent. If these demands are not met, then the funds the councils are said to need desperately will not be made available. Realism suggests that they cut their losses and agree to the donors' terms.

At this point history may well repeat itself. Early in the story of the ecumenical response to poverty, national councils of churches were shaped to meet the needs of the Northern churches and agencies. Projects had to be assessed and the agencies needed channels for their aid. In a discussion about projects at the Swanwick consultation in 1966, for example, proposals were put forward to deal with "the present weakness of many NCCs", partly by encouraging their member churches to support them and partly by offering help from outside: "The strengthening of staff for more effective dealing with projects may well demand additional support from the oikoumene."[3] Then as now NCCs were supported and shaped as instruments of the North, equipped to do what the North required. Then as now they were potentially diverted from an holistic task to a specialized task, from what they might have done if left to themselves to what they did do at the behest of others. Then as now funding and capacity-building from the North made the support of the local member churches more difficult to win and self-reliance more difficult to achieve. Then as now councils of churches co-operated half-approving since there was aid and development work to be done for which funds were needed, half-disapproving of being dictated to and diverted, however benevolently, by outside forces. They came to terms, if reluctantly, with the power of the donors.

But if realism is the way forward it has yet another step to take. Of the many reasons why partnerships do not work — lack of time to foster them, practical pressures, differences of culture and approach — one remains fundamental: the fact that the partners remain "asymmetrical", as "Discerning the Way Together" describes them. They are unequal rather than mutual because they are and always will be undermined by the global imbalance of resources of which the ecumenical imbalance is but a tiny part. And this gap between the rich and the poor is not diminishing but growing. Although this does not rule out people treating one another with a measure of respect, it does make partnership as it is so often described virtually impossible. To quote "Discerning the Way Together": "Money generates power and dependence generates resentment." There is a direct causal link between unequal resources and difficult relationships, which is why simply cutting down the number of partnerships which agencies and their Southern partners attempt to sustain is unlikely to change very much at all. Realism suggests that equal partnership will remain a dream for as long as unequal access to the earth's resources remains a fact.

The ecumenical family must be extremely cautious about pursuing what will always be vitiated. The quest for "partnership", "ecumenical resource-sharing", "ecumenical discipline" or simply "ecumenism" tends to be over-preoccupied with achieving the kind of internal relations which are jeopardized from the start by the context in which they are pursued. The realistic and therefore the more "Christian" alternative is a threefold strategy. First, to be clear that the main aim is to shift or share out more justly global resources rather than ecumenical ones. This must be the acid test applied to projects and programmes, movements, organizations and advocacy. Will they contribute to shifting resources from the rich to the poor? Second, to deploy (rather than "share") our very limited ecumenical resources as strategically as we know how to that end, acting together or separately according to common agreements. Third, to forge alliances, make working agreements, draw up and sign contracts (avoiding the language of partnership) between North and South, rich and poor counterpart organizations, which stand or fall on whether or not they see some part of the strategy through. To say that both partners, North and South, will have something to contribute to such agreements is true. To say they are equal is romantic. The poor sell their souls not when they bow to an unequal relationship in giving and receiving or even in decision-making, but when they agree to cooperate where they do not believe the overall strategy will be advanced.

Relationships then will tend towards the instrumental, designed to get things done, rather than the idealistic, aspiring to ways in which human beings ought to live together especially as a Christian community but which are not possible given the world as it is.

The debate about partnership has sometimes been presented as a dilemma or choice between ecumenism and efficiency. Ecumenism, we are told, requires us to respect the special relationship which binds together the ecumenical family through thick and thin, and to choose to stay with ecumenical partners even where they are judged to be less than efficient when it comes to aid and development and the struggle against poverty and for life. Efficiency, it is said, declares that our first loyalty is to the poorest of the poor and that we must work with whoever we judge will most effectively address our overriding concern, whether they are ecumenical partners or not. The dilemma is not easily resolved. But we must make every effort to achieve what might be called ecumenical efficiency or efficient ecumenism. It is not ecumenism for its own sake any more than it is partnership for its own sake. It commits us instead to do all we can to use ecumenical resources to shift global resources, and to fashion ecumenical instruments among others for shifting them as effectively and efficiently as we can.

One other aspect of the partnership debate is picked up by "Discerning the Way Together". Much of the debate assumes that partners are institutions — councils of churches, agencies or non-governmental organizations (NGOs) — and it mistakenly assumes that relationships between institutions can be modeled on personal relationships. Formally constituted corporate bodies cannot behave like individual people or aspire to the almost intimate relationships that partnership language implies. Institutions, with their necessary procedures and bureaucracies, will find it doubly difficult to embody the ideal of mutuality, and it is thus doubly important for them to be realistic.

But "Discerning the Way Together" asks about the people behind these institutions. Southern contributors questioned the NGOs in the South about how far they speak for the people and the people's movements they claim to represent and whether or not they serve the people's interests. Similar questions are raised within the ecumenical family as to how far councils of churches represent member churches and their local congregations. From the agency point of view, Christian Aid recently discovered that although it was created by the churches to enable them to respond to the challenge of world poverty, it did not enable and support the people in the churches all that well.[4] In general, people felt disabled and overwhelmed by the enormity of the task and the demands being made of them.

In the end the partners in the struggle against poverty are not just the institutions, and not even primarily the institutions, no matter how necessary institutions may be. The primary partners are people in local churches and communities in both North and South, who are sometimes distanced from each other rather than brought more closely in touch by "professional" agencies thinking they know best. Perhaps agencies, councils of churches and NGOs have been too busy discussing their own partnerships when they ought to have been discussing those of the people they are created to serve. Local congregations do not necessarily know best, any more than agencies, but it is worth seeking legitimate ways to put people in touch across the divides of the world and afford them the opportunity to give and receive in the mutuality which is less possible and less relevant at the institutional level. Has the key insight of Larnaca 1986 — that Christian service belongs essentially to the local church and at the level of highly personal, people-to-people relationships — yet been taken seriously into account?

Empowerment

Both "Discerning the Way Together" and "Ecumenical Diakonia" are clear about the need for structural change. If poverty is to be eradicated, the underlying causes, rooted in the way the world is organized, must be removed. The best that "Discerning the Way Together" can say of the present neo-liberal free market system is that it doubts its ability to overcome poverty. The prospects for creating wealth, let alone redistributing it, are not bright. At worst it sees the system as entirely given over to the gods of individualism, selfishness and competition. It requires all too many people to be sacrificial victims. They must remain poor and pay the price so that a minority can grow rich. This unjust order of things must be transformed into a global resource-sharing system.

What seems equally clear, however, is that the system is here to stay. Those who run it have an almost fundamentalist faith in its power to set the world right. Those who vote them into power seem unwilling to vote for anything else. Free-market capitalism has triumphed. Evidence of its success in overcoming poverty and creating productive economies is found in "Asian Tigers" and "Newly Industrialized Countries" like South Korea, Thailand and Taiwan. With the collapse of communism and the loss of confidence in socialism and the programmes of the left, there appears to be no alternative and no need for one. The system which the ecumenical family insists must be changed only tightens its grip, despite our attempts to be strategic and in solidarity with one another.

If the analysis is correct, one consequence is that occasions of desperate need calling for immediate relief are likely to remain as familiar features of the landscape. Whereas the imagined scenario at one stage of ecumenical history was to move from relief to development, it will not now be possible to leave behind disasters and emergencies and refugee crises in that way — if it ever was. They are more than likely to grow in number or in size or both and to deepen. The reasons for such crises are many. Conflict and environmental degradation are prominent among them. But underlying all such factors is the completely indefensible failure to distribute the world's resources, taking too much from one place and forcing those who are left there to deplete further and fight over the little that remains. Such dynamics are far more likely to be continued than to be reversed under the present system.

Two consequences are said to follow. First, an emergency can be so large in scale that it rapidly outstrips the capacity of local organizations, including the churches. They do not have the wherewithal to cope. They may in any case be overwhelmed by it themselves. It requires the ecumenical family to organize itself to move in and take sensitive and supportive, but also far more direct and effective action — often referred to as "operational". Second, the vast majority of emergencies cannot be seen as unfortunate interruptions to the mainstream, ongoing work of development. They are not abnormal; they are normal for as long as the present non-distributive economic system lasts. If at one time emergency work took great care to incorporate the principles of development, avoiding dependency and heading as rapidly as possible towards self-reliance and rehabilitation, development work must now incorporate measures to prepare the poor for the almost inevitable disasters that will continue to come their way. It must plan for setbacks. It must develop strategies for survival as well as for advance. [5]

A third consequence of the persistence of disaster and emergency situations is that the ecumenical family should be unapologetic about offering relief or "aid" to people who will live and die long before the systems which create the emergencies and keep people poor are changed. This immediate response to human need is easily thrown on the defensive. It can be criticized for dealing with symptoms and not causes, for changing nothing and for being a fairly cheap way by which the better-off can ease their consciences. All of this may be true. But it is not the whole truth, and it does not remove the need or the duty to feed the hungry today and not tomorrow. Such compassion, often costly and courageous, cannot be automatically dismissed as mere charity.

Perhaps more than anything else, this sense of having to come to terms with the status quo in the form of an entrenched economic order shifts the debate about empowerment. The change that seems to be required is not just a matter of empowering people in a different way, for example, by giving them the power of the vote in the new democracies instead of the power of organized people's movements or even the power of the gun. Some ways of empowering, such as community-organizing, will remain the same. The change now required is much more a matter of empowering people for a different purpose. Some describe it as moving from liberation to reconstruction. With the old oppressors overthrown — at least in some countries — new and more democratic societies must now be built, and the poor given the opportunity to build them.

There may be a better way of describing the change of purpose, especially if we are correct in believing that the present order of things is here to stay for the foreseeable future. Empowerment is no longer designed to overthrow the system, taking the mighty from their thrones, taking over the seats of the powerful and replacing the system with another. Empowerment is rather for exploiting the system and surviving within it. Strategies for change must give way to strategies for survival. They must be at least as useful for survival and for wresting out of the system what people can get as they must be promising for change.

Gaining access for poor people to markets or extending the markets to include them is one of the newer forms of empowerment. By definition this is a way of changing the system, since it would otherwise leave them out. At the same time, it accepts the system. It comes to terms with the market. It looks for ways in which the poor can produce and sell and gain credit so that they can benefit from the market as it now exists.

Organizing people is a more traditional form of empowerment. If people work together there is some hope that they may be able to stand, whereas separate they will certainly fall. "Discerning the Way Together" believes organization needs to be extended beyond local groups, creating networks of churches and other organizations and a lively and varied civil society with national influence. It is a form of changing the system, giving a voice and a platform to those who would otherwise be ignored. But equally it makes use of the growing space within the system to campaign and negotiate and to claim from governments whatever benefits and legal rights it can, including better health care, roads and schools.

For example, the National Campaign Against Hunger in Brazil provides millions of people with food. It helps them to survive. But it has also mobilized vast numbers of people from all social groups in a joint effort in favour of the poor. It has revived solidarity in the midst of unprecedented individualism. It has defied selfishness and greed as the driving forces of the system in favour of a more traditional culture of community and cooperation. [6]

The need to claim benefits and rights partly inspires the emphasis of "Discerning the Way Together" on advocacy in the South, which agencies have supported far less than in the North. Advocacy is often associated with campaigning about the global issues that make people poor, such as trade and debt. But it has the double character of drawing attention to the needs of people within the system and how they could be met, as well as setting out to change it. It gives people the power both to cry out against the structures that harm them in North and South and to ask for what they need to go on struggling for as long as the structures persist.

Self-reliance and sustainability as forms of empowerment implicitly accept the system. They recognize that people have extremely limited resources and that the situation is unlikely to change. They set out to devise ways in which poor people can use whatever is to hand that is productive, sustaining and sustainable (in agriculture, for example) in order to survive. They discover how people can live as far as possible within their resources, since new ones of any great significance are unlikely to come their way. But this ability or power to be self-sufficient is also a strategy for changing the system by building up self-reliant pockets of resistance less beholden to the market and less vulnerable to its power. It is one context in which "Discerning the Way Together" accepts the need for the agencies to pay far more attention to income-generating projects that are not forever relying on outside funding or renewed credit.

Empowering people to exploit systems as much as to change them is controversial. Many of the Southern contributors to "Discerning the Way Together" can be read as being strongly against it. For them this is the time "to be excluded from the present order" and to build an "international civil society" outside organized society as we know it. Their anti-systemic approach is not against all systems as such but is firmly opposed to this one "which produces and excludes the poor at the same time". They are also suspicious of a possible shift by Northern agencies away from a clear commitment to transformation towards a more pragmatic attack on poverty. There is a fine line between playing by Western rules — adopting Western tactics and Western efficiency — in order to "beat the system" and being finally co-opted into it.

The danger against which these Southern voices warn is real enough — all of Christian history teaches how difficult it is to be *in* the world but not *of* it — but there are counter-arguments. If such an approach is regarded as little more than compromise and betrayal, settling for what is rather than for what ought to be, it could also be said that not doing what is possible to bend the system in favour of the poor is equally to betray them, especially if no alternative strategy is on offer. The Southern contribution recognizes along with the North that "people are looking for practical answers to their daily problems, even when structural problems or root causes have not been resolved".

Another counter-argument is that it is not at all clear what opting out of the system into an alternative "international civil society" would mean. Does it mean modifying the system with a bias towards subsidiarity and self-reliance? Does it mean building well-connected and mutually supportive international networks? Does it mean being forthright and persistent in exposing the demonic nature of the economic order? Does it mean not being reverential and not allowing hoped-for favours to silence criticism? All these are ways of being anti-systemic, for all the risks of compromise which go with them, and at times these sorts of tactics appear to be what is in mind. But if being anti-systemic means that agencies and churches in North and South are to opt out of the system altogether, no longer taking resources from governments and financial institutions like the World Bank and using them as best they can in the interests of the poor, no longer engaging constructively with those who shape and run the systems in an attempt to modify them in the interests of the poor, but rejecting them wholesale, would it actually enhance the ability to bring about change? Or would it simply be a rather empty gesture of principle, leaving them marginalized with even fewer resources and less influence and thus less potential for good?

Theology

The Southern contribution to "Discerning the Way Together", some of it echoed in "Ecumenical Diakonia", actually does some theology rather than merely discussing how to do it. For example, it is highly critical of the present economic order as "sacrificial" in a way that is entirely unacceptable from a Christian point of view. Christianity affirms suffering and sacrifice when it is self-giving and redemptive, expressing a willingness to serve and love in a costly way for the healing of the world's pain. It is exemplified in the sacrifice of Christ. But Christianity is not willing to accept that the lives of some human beings, in this case the poor of the earth, are expendable or fit to be "sacrificed" to satisfy the avarice of others.

Again, the Southern contributors to "Discerning the Way Together" are clear that the Christian faith is "anti-systemic" by nature. This is not to say that it is against all systems — social, political, economic or whatever — but that every system is by definition open to question. First, it is a *human* system, with all the inevitable limitations which that implies. It cannot take every need or every eventuality into account or solve every problem. Second, it is a *sinful* system, because the men and women who construct and maintain it not only have limited insights and capacities but also have vested interests. Fearful as they are, they are out to protect and to benefit themselves. They are not equally committed to the good of all. Such theological insights, based on the Christian understanding of human nature, should produce caution and scepticism in relation not only to existing systems but also to anything that takes their place. They should most certainly challenge the fundamentalism which sometimes surrounds the present economic order.

That having been said, "Discerning the Way Together" displays much the same lack of confidence when it comes to theology as we have seen in so much of the ecumenical family's response to poverty. This shows through at three points in particular. The first is the agencies' nervousness about engaging with other theological traditions that inspire different approaches to the challenge of world poverty and the task of development, which are said to be increasingly influential. The "conservative" or "fundamentalist" tradition is specifically mentioned. This might mean a sectarian and anti-ecumenical approach setting Protestant communities against Catholics for example. It might mean an approach which rejects any serious engagement with the injustices of the present order in favour of escapist hopes for an other-worldly resolution of this world's problems. It might mean the conservative theology that goes with right-wing politics. Less pejoratively, it could mean a theological approach, found in many Pentecostal groups, which takes more seriously the way in which spirituality can in fact sustain people in circumstances unlikely to change much in their lifetime. Or again it could mean a theological approach which looks for a more open and obvious alliance between development and mission, between offering the hungry bread and offering them the gospel which is the bread of life. Only at this point, incidentally, is the classic ecumenical debate about "holism" (discussed in chapter 2 above) in any sense referred to in "Discerning the Way Together".

This reluctance to join in debate with those who take a very different theological stance may be due to a feeling on the part of the ecumenical agencies that it would be largely unproductive. It may be due to a failure to recognize how destructive conservative influences could be in a world where we need common ground between peoples of different faiths and traditions rather than a polarized debate. It may be born of the feeling that there is as much to gain as to oppose in these other approaches. It rather assumes that such encounters must be antagonistic; but there is little chance of reinvigorating our faith and theology without them.

The chief explanation of the reluctance to engage probably relates to a second point at which a lack of confidence is seen, namely in the admission that agencies lack the resources for engaging in theological reflection. This is frankly admitted in the response of the four directors:

> A radical scepticism with regard to the present neo-liberal model of development, and an insistence on the importance of theology, emerged from both the Northern and Southern reports as interrelated and fundamental issues. Important as they are, such issues are well beyond the present capacities of the agencies to respond to in any adequate way. Here agencies look to the churches to undergird our work with critical and creative thinking on Christian approaches to the economic order.

Third, if agencies are to engage in the pastoral cycle of theological reflection on practice and practice in the light of theological reflection, the problem of methodology remains. Agencies must gain confidence first in asking the three basic questions (see chapter 5 above) about what they are dealing with, what they want to achieve and how to achieve it; and then in trawling the Bible and the traditions of the churches for relevant insights and using them (along with those of other disciplines) to nourish their thinking as they make up their minds about the next appropriate steps to take.

Finally, it is feared that the theological approaches of the ecumenical agencies themselves and their different opinions as to how any theology relates to development are so diverse that any consensus would be extremely difficult to achieve. If one of the objects of the exercise is "discerning the way *together*", different internal approaches to the implications of Christian faith may not prove all that unifying.

Despite this lack of confidence, the importance of doing theology is not called into question but underlined. Several arguments are advanced as to why more should be done while acknowledging that in general it remains peripheral within the agencies.

Is it possible for this debate about theology not to become, like the debate about partnership, another case of endlessly aspiring to an ideal which cannot be fulfilled? Here are three suggestions.

First, if the agencies lack the resources to do the theology which they believe to be important for their work, they must take steps to obtain these resources. The most obvious direction in which to look is to those who have more confidence — not that they have all the answers — in relating faith to the issues and challenges and questions with which world poverty confronts us. Agencies need to build good working relations with the individuals and institutions that possess such confidence. In the North, for example, there is a flourishing tradition of Christian social ethics. It could play a significant role in relating faith to development; and it is pursued as a discipline by people who believe they know what they are about. Why is there so little contact at a working level between them and the practitioners? Or again, if there is scant interest in the North in an expression of Christian faith, mission and obedience which focuses on the concern of a Christ-like God for the poor of the earth, that is certainly not true of the churches of the South. Liberation and contextual theologies, the base Christian communities, associations of Third World theologians, kairos documents, to mention but a few examples, demonstrate that the resources and the confidence are there. Agencies are supposed to be skilled at making links. Why then are so few links made at a working level to ensure that the theologies of the South are used to inform the policies, programmes and procedures of the North?

Second, there is an understandable but somewhat vicious circle that has to be broken. In general the engagement of the Northern churches with world poverty has come to be seen as a fairly specialized, professional and technical affair. As a result, the technical and professional qualifications and practical experience of staff members are rated more highly than whether or not they are people of active Christian faith or members of local congregations. It is agreed that many of the jobs that need to be done can be done perfectly well regardless of a person's religious commitments. But if those employed by the agencies are there more by virtue of their professional and technical abilities than by virtue of their Christian commitments, it is inevitable that they will see less and less reason for bringing faith and theological reflection into their work. They will only reinforce the perception of a technical rather than theological enterprise and begin to go round the "vicious" circle all over again.

To say that the circle should be broken could be heard as discounting the need for professional and technical expertise or as wrongly suggesting that theology is equally relevant at every level of work — which it is not — or as implying that people who are not practising Christians will not be so good at their jobs in either a technical or moral sense as those who are. No such implications necessarily follow.

Breaking the circle means making a choice. On the one hand, development agencies, like banks and industrial enterprises, can be seen as highly specialized, working largely within their own autonomous disciplines and defined in those terms. This does not make theological considerations irrelevant. We always need to be asking about their purposes, about the motives of those involved, about the values being upheld and their effects on human communities. But we shall not forever demand that as institutions they do theology. Instead, the church will want to expose them from time to time to its own theological critique from the outside, and support with good opportunities for reflection and formation those Christian individuals who feel called to work in them.

On the other hand, Christian agencies which are called to enable the churches to make the best possible response to poverty could, like mission agencies, be seen as "faith communities" in which it is only to be expected that Christian believers, committed to the church (though not uncritical of it), active in worship and Christian witness and service, will be very much in evidence. Precisely because of their faith, they do not have to be urged continuously to take faith into account. They see the point of taking it into account, and want to discover how best to do so in order to be true to what they claim to believe. Only then does theological reflection cease to be an unreasonable and unnecessary duty and become a matter of their own integrity and self-expression.

Third, we have already argued that theological reflection is unlikely to gain much ground until people are convinced that Christian faith is actually talking about the real live issues that they face and has relevant and useful contributions to make. The language of the questions they ask and the language of the responses they seek from theology have to be the same. In a sense, theology has to prove that it is worth doing. Nothing will change very much until theology becomes attractive and useful rather than a question of duty or integrity.

In this connection those who plead the cause of theology should take note of a number of puzzling contemporary issues that agencies and others have to face and seize their chance to demonstrate what help theology and theologians can offer in supporting and shaping the ecumenical response to poverty. Out of many I mention three.

The first is the question of the persistence of poverty. It is surprising how seldom this is seen in the ecumenical documents as cause for a fundamental challenge to faith in a powerful God of love and to traditional Christian explanations of why there is so much suffering in the world (technically referred to by the theologians as "theodicies"). But beyond that we are confronted with the question as to *why* poverty persists. Is it because we do not know, even in the modern world, how to be rid of it? Or is it because we know how to be rid of it but lack what is often referred to as the "political will" to do so? And if it is a matter of the will, what is the likely explanation and what if anything can be done about it?

Several theological "explanations" are to hand. Some refer to "the powers of this dark world" which are greater and stronger than our human power, individual or collective, and to which we are enslaved. Others talk about human disobedience. We deliberately choose to ignore the claims of God and of justice, or the rules for taking proper care of the earth and its resources. Still others deepen the question and ask *why* we disobey or act in self-serving and destructive ways. Is it sheer perversity or is it fear which warps our lives and drives us to short-sighted measures of self-protection?

A coherent theological answer to such questions is important and potentially productive. There is little point in persistently exhorting people to do what they persistently refuse to do or in expecting the world to change its behaviour on demand. We need the best understanding we can arrive at as to why it behaves as it does, so that we can then act accordingly. Helpful responses depend on good analysis. It could well bring to the fore two insights which the response to poverty has tended to ignore. One is the fundamental human need for security: it is difficult to care for others if we do not feel reasonably safe or taken care of ourselves. We behave badly largely out of fear. The other has to do with the more personal and spiritual dimensions of material wealth and poverty and their actual and perceived relationships to the quality of our lives.

A second area in which theology could be of help is on the question of compromise. We have talked about the need to empower the poor to work within exploitative systems rather than overturn them. We have seen how national councils of churches must bow to the pressures of Northern donors if they are to win resources. If we improve structural adjustment policies we may ease the worst of their effects on the poor while taking all too seriously the very economic structures that tend to make them poor. Agencies likewise have to deal with governments and social groups which prosper at the expense of the poor. They must play according to their rules at home and abroad, including the rule that the poor must account in detail to the rich while the rich need give little if any account of themselves to the poor. At a quite different level, the need to find common ground with people of other faiths may require us to soft-pedal some of the more distinctive aspects of our own.

Is this sort of compromise simply storing up trouble for the future, refusing to confront what ought to be confronted now? Is it far too pragmatic and unprincipled, agreeing to whatever may achieve the immediate results we are looking for? Or is it in fact highly principled, in that it looks for the way which will best serve our neighbours and reap the most benefit for the poor, and so acts out of the kind of Christian love which goes beyond sentiment to maximizing the good of those it claims to love. Some sorting out as to what is the moral high ground and what is the slippery slope, of how Christian compromise is saved from being mere co-optation, of how we can live effectively in the world and not become merely part of it, of the merits and weaknesses of what are called idealism and realism, of how to compromise with a good conscience — all of this could be extremely supportive of the contemporary debate about development, where instead of turning the world upside-down there seem to be plenty of reasons for coming to terms with it more or less as it is.

Third, theology might help us to seize the opportunity provided by
the current interest in ideology, values, culture and civil society to win
wider acceptance and support for the institutional churches as serious
players in the field of development, worthy of public support. Up to
now churches have been suspect as reliable partners in development
precisely because of their interest in some of these matters. Rather
than promoting economic growth they could be peddling a faith and
busy proselytizing. Rather than serving society in general they could
be strengthening their own institutions. But the understanding of
development has widened and deepened. The values and beliefs which
hold communities together (or drive them apart) and inform their ways
of doing things, and the cultural patterns and rituals which bind them
to one another, have to be treated just as seriously as any techniques
for agriculture or health care when improving the quality of life. And
"participation" is everything, not only through the ballot box but
through the institutions of civil society, including voluntary organizations, trade unions and churches, where people can belong and have a
sense of ownership and can contribute and have their say. This richer
understanding of development coincides with a good deal of talk about
holism within the ecumenical family. But what is required is a
theological account of the church which, rather than merely echoing
or conforming to what is being said about development, shows where
the tasks of the church and the aims of development legitimately
converge and can be mutually supportive. Running right through the
church's rituals and training programmes, synods and councils and
institution-building, as well as through its service and witness in the
world, could be the desire to promote the human values, responsive
and self-reliant people and strong participatory communities and
institutions which the development world could now welcome and
support across the board. But such a holistic theology of mission
needs careful and competent articulation in a fresh *apologia* for the
church.

An imaginative leap

In discussing the future, "Discerning the Way Together" contains
few real surprises. Its proposals remain very much within the familiar
parameters of the debate about aid and development and the ecumenical response to poverty. They feel like inching forward, not leaping

ahead. The recipe is much the same as before even if, as is hoped, much improved. None of this is necessarily cause for criticism. Indeed, short of anything blindingly new, we are required to inch forward as best we can, persevering with what we know rather than giving up or drawing back out of impatience or cynicism. This is the steady, responsible obedience required of us.

It does not however prevent us feeling disappointed and wanting something more. The achievements of the last fifty years are considerable. They are reflected above all in the struggles of poor people themselves and in their abilities, courage and hope. But there remains a huge sense of dismay even for those who have known such people and seen their achievements. At the end of the day, whatever the improvements, the absolute number of poor people in the world is growing. There are more than there were fifty years ago; and the gap between rich and poor is getting wider. The earth's resources continue to flow relentlessly towards those who already have and away from the have-nots.

And if the battle against poverty does not seem to have progressed all that much, neither has the ecumenical response to poverty. We seem to have learned all too little by immersing ourselves in practical obedience and reflecting on our experience. We seem to repeat the same mistakes, as we noted when comparing the record of development agencies with that of missionary societies. We re-invent what our ecumenical memory forgets. The arguments about mission and politics and power and theology, the four themes examined in this book, do not advance all that much. Many of the insights came as early as the days of the International Missionary Council, and are then repeated. Even our inching forward can collapse into the familiar syndrome of the same old issues and attitudes dressed up in new forms.

From time to time the ecumenical documents reflect this sense of dismay. Commenting on the WCC's Nairobi assembly in 1975, David Paton said that there was "nothing specially new in the way of ideas. The ideas and causes were still for the most part those that had erupted at Uppsala or earlier".[7] Ten years later, Harry de Lange concluded that

one of the dangers in the ecumenical social ethics debate is that we repeat ourselves too often, especially in the development discussions. In this respect we mirror the secular debate. The second Brandt Report is more or less a repetition of the first. There is no real progress, and the agenda of UNCTAD VI is almost identical with the agenda of UNCTAD I![8]

Paul Abrecht may be expressing disagreement or this same sense of disappointment in a comment on two books published in 1987 (one by Ulrich Duchrow, the other by Charles Elliott) demanding "radical and new Christian approaches to world economic problems":

> Both claim to build on ecumenical experience... Both omit much of the ecumenical record on economic justice. Both base their proposals for change on ideas, especially with respect to economic ethics, which the ecumenical movement has examined and rejected in the past.[9]

Konrad Raiser, speaking at El Escorial, said bluntly, "Everything that needs to be said has in fact long since been said." The suggestions in the working document "seem to have little more to say about the keyword 'sharing' than what has already figured in recommendations and exhortations to the churches from ecumenical gatherings for many years".[10] Seta Pamboukian of Lebanon, writing in 1994 says: "Since the El Escorial consultation, I believe, we have been repeating ourselves on the subject of diakonia and resource sharing."[11]

One response to this depressing sense of *déjà vu* is found in "Discerning the Way Together" when it calls for the agencies and others to become learning organizations. Their attempts at self-evaluation showed how unpractised they were at drawing on their experience and that of their partners and learning from it. Part of learning is not forgetting. It underlines the importance of historical memory, to which books like this one and careful records and the building up of ecumenical disciplines and ways of doing things which encapsulate and institutionalize hard-won lessons of the past can all make their contributions.

A second response is hinted at by Konrad Raiser. The lack of progress may be caused by something deeper than our lack of ideas or not knowing what to do: "Our theology is right, at least in theory. Why then... so few results...? Have we really understood the causes of the dogged resistance to the necessary changes?"[12] Which takes us back to the earlier plea for more theological work to be done on the persistence of poverty as a spiritual and psychological problem as well as a technical one — work which might in turn foster a more adequate response.

But there is a third response to the sense of disappointment. As well as inching forward and recycling the old and familiar or the half-forgotten, we long for something new and for the imaginative leap forward.

A new theology

For one thing, we long for a new theology, or a new account of our Christian faith taking us beyond the classical, the Western, the evangelical and the liberation theologies of yesterday, none of which seems entirely satisfying today. Some have referred to it as a "vital and coherent theology". Others seek for it in what they call a "theology of life" — though this term says more about how such a theology is arrived at, by reflecting on experience, than what it contains. I believe it has to do fundamentally not with a sinful world that has to be redeemed, nor a world enslaved to principalities and powers that has to be liberated, nor a suffering world that has to be explained and justified, nor an ordered world that has to be conserved or maintained, but with a chaotic, threatening, unformed and frightening disorder which has yet to be "created" or fashioned into a human world by inventive and creative women and men in collaboration with an inventive and creative God.

If that is anything like the case, if we are to understand ourselves as partners in the business of manufacturing or constructing a world, then theology will take a renewed interest not only in imagining what kind of world is to be made but in discovering how best to make it, not in how you set free or forgive or restore or explain things, but how you actually create out of the given materials. It will become fascinated with the strategies and dynamics that characterized the highly creative living and dying of Jesus, and what Christians have thought and written about that in the light of their own creative experiences. It will contemplate with renewed excitement the potential of Christ-inspired participation, inclusion, confrontation, vulnerability and generosity for making the world we have yet to cast eyes on. It will view with a new seriousness not the moral obligation to serve the poorest but the creative strategy of starting at the most neglected and unpromising point with those regarded as unnecessary for any constructive enterprise. The new theology we long for will in this sense be a "practical theology", reflecting on the kind of practice which is most likely to be productive, as much as a "conceptual theology" which offers a meaningful framework for our lives.

The integrity of development

It is tempting to say we need a new concept of development. This has certainly been high on the agenda of the ecumenical family, especially the WCC's programme unit on Sharing and Service, in the mid-1990s. The discussion, understandably, was triggered by disillusionment with the prevailing economic order: with what it had and had not done for the poorest, and with its tendency to reduce human beings to producers and consumers of material goods (*homo economicus*).

The alternative was hinted at in words like community, sustainability (going beyond the standard definition about meeting the needs of the present without denying future generations the wherewithal to meet theirs), participation, inclusion (in a society where everyone is valued and has a role to play) and human dignity. These, rather than mere economic growth, were to define the goal.

The discussion also arose in debates about a more adequate response to emergencies, meeting not only the immediate need for food and shelter but also the psychological and spiritual needs of traumatized people and communities broken by conflict. [13]

The discussion raises a number of issues. First, while it may be relatively easy to persuade the ecumenical family that present development policies have failed, progress towards better ones will depend on changing the minds of others beyond the family who are not so readily convinced. Many in government and international institutions firmly believe that the neo-liberal free-market economy, together with their own efforts to adjust Third World economies so that they can operate more successfully in the global market, are steadily winning the day. If anything needs to be changed it is in the direction of making the same system more responsible with regard to the environment. Otherwise it is a matter of going for growth much as before.

Second, we must clarify what is in fact new in what is being said about an alternative. How does it differ — apart from vocabulary — from what the secular world is saying when it talks about participation, democracy, culture, civil society, social integration, human rights and sustainability?[14] Is it very different from what the ecumenical family has been saying for years about holistic development and the need to address the whole person in community? If not, we should be wary of being diverted from the steady business of inching forward by idle longings for alternative visions.

Third, if the old concept of development has failed, we must be clear about how far attention should be switched from economic considerations to cultural, communitarian and spiritual concerns, and how far we have still to find a better economic system which will do what the present one is failing to do, that is, to generate adequate economic resources for all without exhausting the earth and to see that all get their fair share. The economics may have failed, but economics is still part of development and we must not unwittingly abandon what is difficult terrain for us in favour of the more familiar home ground of theological debate.

But fourth, perhaps the most important new work we have to do is not imagining a new concept of development but understanding better the inter-relationships between the different elements of the one we already have. We mentioned in Chapter 2 one way of understanding these interrelationships and the doubts that have been cast upon it. Economic development can be seen as the necessary base or foundation on which the edifice of a rounded, well-developed human community can be built, and without which the whole enterprise is doomed from the start. This economic base is for outside agencies to help provide. The edifice should be left to the community to design and complete. But can the two be thought of in such a sequential way or be separated out into discrete compartments?

The task is to understand what might be called "the integrity of development", the complex inter-connections which must be appreciated and respected if we are going to manage development well for the good of all.

Most examples quoted tend to be negative and one-sided. Capitalism was once thought to resonate with the Protestant ethic and the secular city of God. Now economic development by way of the neoliberal free-market system is criticized for destroying communities. It replaces human cooperation with the kind of competition which has scant regard for the dignity of human beings and the social bonds between them.[15] This may be true, but the "integrity of development" is far more complex and interesting than that. What kind of economic growth, for example, enhances community and what kind of community fosters a successful economy? What forms of economic activity are likely to prove themselves productive and satisfying within a particular culture? Once basic human needs are addressed, what is the correlation of happiness and well-being with rising income and consumption? How can participation rather than authoritarianism promote efficiency? Can the age-old tensions between the devolved and the centralized, competition and cooperation, individual enterprise and community, freedom and order, rights and responsibilities be resolved?

The fact is that there is a dynamic interplay between economic, ecological, social, cultural, moral and spiritual development. We know little about how they can be mutually supportive and sustaining. The answer is unlikely to be the same for every community or culture, any more than what is satisfying and fulfilling is the same for every individual. The relationship between the arrangements we make for our common life at the global level and for our varied communities at a more local level then becomes of crucial importance. Can we live together in one world but live differently in our inter-dependent communities?

The Northern contribution to "Discerning the Way Together" has little to say about a new concept of development. For good or ill, it found the existing one, with its economic, social and cultural goals "reaffirmed and widely shared between North and South". It does have a good deal to say about "alternative visions". Its main suggestions have to do with "people-friendly markets and people-friendly governments"; with the need for participation and civil society if states are to work better for people. But it also talks about a "strengthened system of global governance" which prevents decisions being taken only by a small group of rich nations. This quite properly reintroduces the issue of justice.

Any alternative global order has to allow separate communities room to breathe, so that they can pursue their own development in an holistic and integrated way as well as having some way of resisting what other self-interested parties will otherwise impose upon them.

The huge, sometimes "global" distances between people who trade with each other and thereby depend on each other and decide about each other may have the effect of making injustice all that easier to live with and maintain. While being close carries no guarantees, I remain attracted to a strong bias towards (though not wholesale adoption of) economic and political "subsidiarity", in which local communities and local people, especially the communities of the poor, take as many matters as they can into their own hands. [16]

New institutions

Besides a new theology and a new understanding of development, many feel the need for new institutions. It is certainly difficult to see how existing institutions can take on board some of the contemporary challenges, let alone longstanding issues. In the first place, the ecumenical enterprise is fuelled for good or ill by Northern institutions with the ability to win resources from public appeals and from governments as well as from the churches. Those resources are now under threat, and competition for them is growing. For how much longer will fund-raising donor agencies make sense as the main instruments of the ecumenical war against poverty?

Second, just as the missionary movement had to replace the scenario of a movement from North or West to South with that of "mission in six continents", so development institutions with mandates largely relating to poverty in the South have to come to terms with a phenomenon which is now everywhere and can no longer be defined in geographical terms. "Discerning the Way Together", following Larnaca eight years earlier, challenged the agencies to take more account of poverty in the North.

Third, world poverty requires a global strategy as well as a highly personal and intimate approach. But getting the various players, even within the ecumenical family, to cooperate and act strategically remains a massive if not impossible task, given their different mandates and ways of working and the different demands and expectations of their various constituencies. Many attempts have been and still are made to be strategic. They include the WCC's efforts at regionalization, in which the ecumenical family comes together to strategize at regional and national levels; its experiments with lead agencies; joint ventures and policy papers; ecumenical disciplines in which even separate actions take on a common aim and character; and the good intentions of exercises like "Discerning the Way Together". All of these ventures demonstrate just how difficult it is, not to mention time-consuming and expensive. The debate about global governance now needs its counterpart within the world of ecumenical relations.

Fourth, the classic ways of working within the ecumenical family are coming under increasing pressure. Traditionally, the agencies have not generally been "operational". Rather than directly carrying out programmes in the South, they have supported the programmes of local churches, councils and other organizations. Traditionally, the agencies have not generally been present to any great extent on a permanent basis in Third World countries. That at least has been the ideal, fiercely supported once again by the Southern participants in "Discerning the Way Together". Various factors, from the scale of emergencies to the preference of Northern governments for dealing with agencies that take a "hands-on" approach and for funding Southern NGOs more directly, have put traditional ways of working and the institutions which are shaped accordingly under increasing threat.

Fifth, the debate about holism and the relation between mission and development has always seemed easier to resolve theologically than institutionally. Despite the debate, separate institutions for mission and development still remain, and the mismatch between councils of churches and development agencies, with all the accompanying tensions and misunderstandings, is likely to continue, unless of course the councils are once again shaped to the requirements of the North. The Northern agencies have a narrower agenda than the churches but a wider circle of counterpart organizations with which they believe they must cooperate. One solution is to multiply the number of specialized, professional church development agencies in the South to match those of the North. At that point we would be bound to ask again whether at such a level of specialization any of them, South or North, would need to be labelled as "Christian" (any more than a credit bank or an agricultural institute) or be the responsibility of the churches as such. The challenge that might then remain for the churches would be to create something like an ecumenical council for world mission, modelled on some of the more enterprising bilateral or confessional world bodies, designed to deploy all kinds of resources for a strategic, holistic task within the framework of a fresh account of Christian faith and mission and hope.

Institutions find it notoriously difficult to tell when their time has come; and it is rarely possible to clear the ground completely and start again. The upshot may therefore be continuing, patient and responsible efforts to adapt existing institutions, inching forward here as elsewhere. The longing for something new nevertheless remains.

The ecumenical family, even when narrowly defined as we have tended to do, can boast an international network — global, regional, national, local — that is the envy of many another international organization. The ecumenical family also knows that it has to deal with "globalization", a highly integrated global economy, if it is to make a relevant response to poverty in the contemporary world. To some extent it must deal with globalization on global terms, as a global institution that can engage with and take on other global institutions in the struggle for a fairer sharing out of the world's resources. But it must also deal with globalization on anything but its own terms, offering the marginalized and excluded in North and South the means of being in touch with each other across the world and of being included in circles of mutual support and cooperation.

The ecumenical family has the means to do both. The tragedy will be if it does neither — because it is too busy sorting out its institutional arrangements for its own high-minded internal reasons rather than in order to face up to the external challenges; because it has neither the wit nor the wisdom to see that the members of the family in North and South, churches and agencies, rich and poor and not-so-poor, are on the same side more than on opposite sides; because it insists on mutuality to the detriment of partnership; because it tends to divide the common task rather than enabling an inevitably divided family to do it together. It is here that signs of hope can be seen in such new institutional arrangements as Action of Churches Together (ACT), set up by the ecumenical family in 1995 as a new way of responding to emergencies, pooling the resources of North and South, agencies and churches, international and local organizations in a single efficient, well-coordinated ecumenical instrument. Similar signs of hope may be seen in the agreement between Nordic agencies and churches and agencies in Southern Africa to sink some of their differences and work together on planning, funding, implementing, managing and accounting for projects and programmes. [17]

On being creative

"Inching forward" and "imaginative leaps" recall the contrast made by Jürgen Moltmann between two kinds of future. [18] One kind, extrapolated from the present, draws out the implications and the possibilities of what now exists as sensibly as it can. It moves essentially within existing parameters and processes. It can be forecast and calculated. It grows. It might be seen as "inching forward". The second kind of future is imagined or "anticipated". It is beyond what is previously known. It transcends it, disrupts it, challenges it, makes it look tired and old by comparison. It is wished for, longed for. Rather than prolonging present conditions, it sounds like "making all things new". It might have something to do with our own longings for fresh starts in the face of our disappointments. It is an attractive and seductive possibility.

The contrast between these futures needs handling with care. No one doubts that from time to time we experience what is totally new. There are great leaps forward. But we can do little consciously about them. We can only long and hope and wait for them and, if they come, regard them as God's gifts or welcome surprises. If we ourselves are to be creative and make a future we cannot create like that, out of nothing. We can only make a future out of what we have. God's future may be Moltmann's so-called "anticipated" future. Ours is more likely to be "extrapolated" — though no less Christian for that.

Nor should the two futures — "inching forward" and "being imaginative" — be regarded as mutually exclusive. Moltmann agrees, though he is especially concerned that the second not be downplayed: "A social policy... does not result from a calculable and extrapolated future alone, nor from ethical maxims and wishes alone. It results from a combination of what man knows and can do with what man hopes and desires." He adds that if the future is only calculated it perpetuates present power structures, since only those with the power to implement can meaningfully make it. [19] We need both to imagine and to calculate, and we are capable of both. Just as imagination, brainstorming, parallel thinking, dreaming may cast fresh light on old problems, so paying careful attention to what already exists, worrying away at it and not giving up, can eventually lead to a breakthrough and reap its rewards. Both God's future and ours may learn from the past and build on experience.

Even more important, perhaps, is a refusal to confine "creativity" to the radically new. We need to be just as imaginative and creative in adapting and rearranging the familiar for the sake of the poor as in dreaming of totally new possibilities. We need to be just as imaginative and creative over institutional and intellectual and practical details as in conjuring up grand schemes and ideas. We should not simply yearn for something completely different but for imaginative patience all round.

Nothing can guarantee that we shall be creative about the ecumenical response to poverty. Nothing can guarantee that we shall make progress or see things differently or open up to fresh possibilities or even spiral ahead instead of going around in circles. Being creative is not a mechanical procedure or an exact science. But if it cannot be guaranteed or organized, there are good reasons for thinking it can be fostered.

Radical participation

At several points, of which participation is one, the insights of the biblical tradition and Christian teaching and the lessons learned from experience combine to suggest how we are most likely to move forward in our quest for an end to poverty and to a more human world or the kingdom of God — in other words, how to be creative. At the same points, the pastoral cycle or theological reflection on practice not only offers us good reasons for what we are doing and high ideals, but actually contributes to its contents. It has things to say not only about the whys and wherefores of the ecumenical response to poverty, but about how we should actually set about it (the third of our three basic questions when it comes to hard thinking).

There are many remarkable and interesting features of the ministry of Jesus. They are glimpsed rather than systematized in the gospel stories. One was his determination to include in the society of his day and in his own creative work those whom the conventional in-crowd thought were best left out of the reckoning. This determination to include has been obscured, perhaps deliberately, by portraying his radical invitations as acts of "forgiveness", so much so that it is almost as if Jesus went along with popular opinion instead of challenging it! To dismiss as "sinners" the people left out — the blind, the beggar, the harlot, the outcast, the leper and the tax-collector — was a handy way to justify their exclusion. They deserved to be left out — a sentiment we are all too ready to echo regarding the poor of today's earth and the contemporary leper, especially the poor and the lepers on our own doorstep, who probably cause us more immediate unease than those who are a long way away. The truth is and was that they are no more sinners (and no less) than anybody else, and are no more in need of forgiveness than anybody else. Insiders and outsiders are much the same in this respect.

Jesus' acts of so-called forgiveness were in fact acts of inclusion: of sitting down at table with those whom most people would never even dream of inviting; of signing up those whom others would never employ; of treating as subjects what others treat as undesirable objects; of saying not "we cannot do with them" but "we cannot do without them". His remarkable suggestion is that there is no practical way to right wrong, build community, discover and travel the road to peace, put an end to the miserable poverty of millions, get ourselves out of the mess we are in without giving a real say and real control and a creative chance to everyone concerned, including the so-called lowest and the least. Such inclusiveness is not simply a moral duty or a piece of idealism. Like putting the last first and the poor on thrones, it is a practical, realistic policy for making a new world.

A very similar note is struck by the accumulated wisdom of the development movement. Often it is given lip-service rather than acted upon, but the truth of it is widely recognized. Whether we are talking about active involvement in small-scale projects, or responsibility for peoples' movements and community organizations, or people as subjects and not objects of history, or national or international networks of protest and advocacy, or democracy, or "people-friendly markets", or civil society, little will change for the better and nothing creative will happen unless people participate and those so often left out are included.

Our earlier discussion about theology highlighted why participation is necessary: not just out of respect for people and for justice, but because of our limited and perverted natures as human beings. All of us approach any issue with a partial and partisan point of view. We cannot do everything or know everything. We are heavily conditioned by our cultures, circumstances and experience; and we are constrained and driven by our own self-interests born of fear and insecurity. If anything productive is to come about, and if we are to be released even to a limited extent from the worst of our narrowness and redeemed from our fearful predispositions, then encounters with those whose limitations and perversions are not less than ours but different from ours is an absolute necessity, offering some hope though no guarantee of mutual correction and completion.

We have also suggested in a brief look at the various understandings of ecumenism that somewhere here, in the business of participation, lies the real genius of the ecumenical movement. By definition it seeks to overcome divisions: to unite a divided church, to make one a divided world, to make the many into a whole, to draw together into communities what is separate and apart.

But once again the ecumenical movement must not make this point simply because it is desirable. Unity is not only a matter of reconciling churches and peoples to one another because it is better that way. It is not simply for its own sake. Ecumenism and participation and inclusiveness are profoundly instrumental. They are essential if the kingdom is to be fashioned. They are not the goal of creation, they are the necessary conditions and instruments of creativity.

The ecumenical movement has taken participation seriously. It has tried to give a place to the poor and the powerless. It has also talked about "balance", partly in terms of the marginalized (women and men, people with disabilities, ethnic origin) and partly in terms of different Christian traditions and geography. But it needs to be more radical and thoroughgoing, not just with regard to sharing power and responsibility but with regard to those who are to be involved. There are others to be brought in to a thoughtful, prayerful and active response to poverty, and there are other counterbalances to be achieved.

Five such counterbalances come to mind. One is between the "experts" and the "people". We understand the point when it comes to the laity and the ordained; less so when it comes to those well-versed in professional disciplines and those without formal qualifications. A second counterbalance is between those who have learned what they know from academic study and those who have learned almost entirely from experience. A third is between the apparently uninfluential and those with powerful positions in governments and banks and transnational corporations and other national and international institutions. While there is always a temptation to write off the powerful as immoral and the powerless as incapable, participation and creativity cannot do without either. A fourth is between the clear-sighted, prophetic, activist campaigners who are convinced they know what has to be done and those who have some practical clues about how to achieve it, given the frustrating but unavoidable realities of bureaucracy, the law, diplomacy and politics. We need hardly add as a fifth the counterbalance among people of different faiths as well as theologies.

There may be no more important task for the ecumenical movement than to organize "radical participation" and so foster the creativity that could make for small steps forward as well as leaps and bounds. No one should underestimate the difficulties of doing so, despite modern communications and our capacity for "globalization" and for creating systems which at the same time affect almost everyone and leave so many people out. It may require new institutions of the ecumenical movement itself. It calls for creative bureaucracy. It certainly underlines the importance of promoting lively exchanges between people who cannot easily meet, of providing inclusive meeting places, of developing the skills which enable participation, of learning from memory and experience the dynamics and logistics of working together (instead of re-inventing the mistakes of the last unproductive occasion) and of agreeing to more adequate criteria than current notions of ecumenical "balance" and populism as to what qualifies as a fully inclusive or participatory enterprise.

Jubilee

Since the occasion for writing this book was a number of fiftieth anniversaries, the word "jubilee" could hardly be avoided. Apart from agencies like Christian Aid and the ecumenical response to poverty, the ecumenical family as a whole celebrates the jubilee of the World Council of Churches in 1998, fifty years after the first assembly in Amsterdam.

Jubilee has often been a matter of "inching forward". Originally it attempted to set up social mechanisms for redistributing the resources that inevitably accrue to the powerful. Today we have to work at the same principle. Debt forgiveness may be an example. Land distribution another. Global and environmental taxes another. And jubilee has always been a matter of "imaginative leaps". The biblical writers and Jesus himself looked for a jubilee year or a year of the Lord's favour that would be quite different from anything so far imagined. It would be a great feast to which all receive invitations, a celebration of all creation, taking possession of Jerusalem, inhabiting a new heaven and a new earth.

And jubilee, whether "inching forward" or as an "imaginative leap", has often been dismissed for never having been put into practice and being unlikely ever to come about. It is written off as an unhelpful, utopian concept. There are good reasons for doing so. Many proposals for jubilee are unrealistic. They simply would not work. The evidence of lasting progress in overcoming poverty and injustice is slight. The teachings of Christian faith itself insist that the kingdom, though present and growing within our history, will be fully realized only beyond it. At best the jubilee, like love, is an impossible possibility. It is always there to question our self-satisfied achievements and call us on to new heights. It is highly useful as a goad but never realizable.

So where does our hope lie? Here is yet another opportunity for theology to prove its worth and help those involved in the ecumenical response to poverty to come to terms with its persistence without at the same time settling for it in a mood of resignation. Too often hope is understood only as a response to the evidence, whether the evidence is the scientific progress which once inspired liberal optimism, or a hard-won if limited victory in the struggle for justice, or stories and rumours of a resurrection from the dead. Things look promising and so we have hope.

But hope may be born not of evidence but of the deliberate commitment of love. It may be because God decides to put God's hope and faith in unpromising and fearful women and men that through costly engagement with them they gradually become more promising. It may be because parents invest their hope in their unpromising offspring that they become more promising. It may be only as with God we decide to hope — and decide to believe that this unpromising world need not stay the same as it is and to engage with it in costly, patient and imaginative ways — that it will become more promising and find it has a future. Hope has as much to do with our commitment as with our reaction to the evidence. We choose to hope.

In 1995, its jubilee year, Christian Aid for the very first time made a statement of faith. It was called "All Shall Be Included". It ended, in hope, like this:

> We long for the time when the meek shall inherit the earth and all who hunger and thirst after justice shall be satisfied; and we believe that despite the persistence of evil, now is always the time when more good can be done and we can make a difference.

NOTES

[1] "Southern Perspectives"; "Report on the Work of Brot für die Welt, Christian Aid, EZE and ICCO"; "The Berlin Minutes"; "Discerning the Way Together — Response of the Four Directors".

[2] See, for example, M.C. Kuchera and K.L. Larsen, "Introducing a Code of Conduct", in *The Ecumenical Review*, Vol. 46, no. 3, July 1994, pp.322-27.

[3] *Digest of the 1966 World Consultation on Inter-Church Aid*, Geneva, WCC, 1966, p.121.

[4] See *The Gospel, the Poor and the Churches*, Social and Community Planning Research and Christian Aid, 1994.

[5] See E. Ferris in *The Ecumenical Review*, July 1994, p.274.

[6] See A. Padilha, *ibid.*, p. 291.

[7] D.M. Paton, ed., *Breaking Barriers*, Geneva, WCC, 1976, p.35.

[8] In *The Ecumenical Review*, Vol. 37, 1985, pp.106-15. This could hardly be said of UNCTAD VIII!

[9] In *The Ecumenical Review*, Vol. 40, 1988, p.147.

[10] In H. van Beek, ed., *Sharing Life*, Geneva, WCC, 1989, p.14.

[11] In *The Ecumenical Review*, Vol. 46, 1994, p.306.

[12] *Loc. cit.*

[13] See E. Ferris, *loc. cit.*, p.273.

[14] On this see J. Borden, *ibid.*, p.314.

[15] Jovili I. Meo cites examples from Pacific communities in *ibid.*, pp.292-99.

[16] See "The Priority of the Poor: A Christian Strategy Reconsidered", *The Epworth Review*, Vol. 21, no. 2, 1994, pp.56-63.

[17] Cf. Kuchera and Larsen, *op. cit.*, pp.322-27; A. Padilha, *op. cit.*, p.290; J. Borden, *op. cit.*, p.315.

[18] See *In Search of a Theology of Development*, Geneva, SODEPAX, 1969, pp.97ff.

[19] *Ibid.*, p.98.

Index

Raiser, K. 28, 156
refugees 1, 2, 11-12, 21, 48, 143
regional groups 10, 60-61, 91, 94
regionalization 10, 60, 93-94, 161
Responsible Society 14, 65-66, 126-27
revolution 9, 14, 59, 66, 68, 71-72,
    88, 119, 128
Roman Catholic 11, 15, 81, 118, see
    also SODEPAX
round tables 10, 13, 40-41, 58, 60-61,
    93, 94, 95

Santa Ana, J. de 102
Search (India) 60
Seoul 70
SODEPAX (Joint Committee on Soci-
    ety, Development and Peace) 15,
    52, 71, 83, 118-23, 126
solidarity 59, 71, 73, 84, 102, 110,
    116, 145
Student Christian Movement (SCM) 5
subsidiarity 147, 161
sustainability 66, 68, 146, 158-59, 160

Tearfund 38

theology 42, 45, 53, 98, Chapter V,
    147-54, 157-58
Timiadis, E. 110
trade 30, 63, 68, 70, 87, 145, 161
transnational corporations 13

Unit II (WCC) 58
Unit III (WCC) 13, 59
Unit IV (WCC) 4, 10, 11, 28, 59
United Nations 1, 8, 11, 58, 109
Urban Rural Mission (URM) 15, 98

Visser 't Hooft, W.A. 5, 23, 56

World Bank 13, 62, 69-70, 90, 147
World Council of Churches (WCC) 1,
    4-6, 8, 14, 27, 37, 45, 49, 57, 62-
    67, 69, 70-72, 81, 83-84, 108,
    155, 168
World Trade Organization 62, 90

YMCA (Young Men's Christian As-
    sociation) 5
YWCA (Young Women's Christian
    Association) 5